A God Promise

McDougal & Associates
Servants of Christ and Stewards of the
Mysteries of God

A God Promise

by

Stephanie Johnson

Published by:

McDougal & Associates
18896 Greenwell Springs Road
Greenwell Springs, LA 70739
www.thepublishedword.com

McDougal & Associates is an organization dedicated to spreading the Gospel of the Lord Jesus Christ to as many people as possible in the shortest time possible.

ISBN: 978-1-950398-34-8

Printed on demand in the U.S., the U.K. and Australia
For Worldwide Distribution

Dedication

I would like to dedicate this book to my Lord and Savior, Jesus Christ. I thank God for allowing me to complete the book. It has truly been a labor of love.

Acknowledgements

Special thanks are due to the following people:

My mother, Shirley: I love you and I thank you for your support and for your silent strength. I pray God continues to bless you with good health and long life. God will reward you for your dedication to Him and to your family.

My daughters, Chanelle Hope and Danielle Faith Johnson: I thank God that you have both made me a proud mother. I'm so happy that you have started your professional careers and that you both are young women of destiny. I know you will continue to be all the Lord has called you to be. I love you both. Always hold up the light and strive for excellence.

My sister Angela and brothers Reginald and Obadiah, and my nieces and nephews: you all know my prayer, that the Father continue to bless our family with salvation, health, and healing and a multitude of blessings, not only for this generation, but for all the generations to come. I pray God's best blessings upon your life and your children's lives.

Contents

He promised me He would take care of me.
He promised me He would provide for me.
He promised me He would never leave me.
He promised me He would never hurt me.
He promised me He would love me forever.
He made me a promise that only God can
make; He made, "A God Promise!"

By Stephanie Johnson, M.Ed.

Foreword by
Mukonda M. Banda

Today, we live in society that imposes its pagan culture on Christians, and if we are not careful, we can be trapped in its ways. Sometimes we forget the promises of God! This book is a reminder of what God has said and what our response to what God said should be. My love and dependence on the promises of God has grown over the years, and I have learned that I can access those promises by faith in God.

Stephanie Johnson is a passionate teacher, leader, mentor, mother, community worker and minister of the Gospel. A lot can be said about her. But the fact is that I have come to know her as a practical Christian who loves to see order in God's Kingdom. Stephanie's goal is to bring awareness of the promises of God, of God as the Promise Keeper and of how to obtain His promises. She shows us what should be our stance in the process of waiting and our life after the promise is fulfilled.

A God Promise

In this book, you can expect encouragement, empowerment, encounters and experiences that will mark your life for positive living. The subject of the promise is very important as it unlocks the blessings that are meant to be experienced by those who, by faith, receive from God. Stephanie explains how God's promises are connected to a life of praise and shows that the confidence embedded in God's nature will lead God's children into higher praise. This is a call to be a God seeker and to learn to walk in God's blessings for our lives. Living your life like you know your heavenly Daddy and that your Daddy is a man of His word.

I pray that this book will not only bless you, but will inspire you to make changes in your life, in order for you to access the promises of God.

Mukonda M. Banda
Exodus Children's Foundation, Zambia

Author's Foreword

A God Promise is a book the Lord had me to write as I was believing Him for many different things myself. At first, it seemed as though the promise was very far off. I encouraged myself by reminding myself of the promises the Lord had kept for me before. I knew that God was and is faithful and that He would surely keep His word.

As I write to you today, I still have promises that I'm waiting to be fulfilled, but I no longer question the Father. I just know that the time for the promise to be fulfilled has not yet arrived. In the meantime, I want to encourage you to wait on the Lord and don't get discouraged as you believe God to see your dreams come true.

The Bible says that waiting develops patience in believers and that we ought to let patience *"have her perfect work."* This means that if you wait, you will be rewarded. Therefore, when you feel yourself growing tired or discouraged or even angry with God, take a step back and remember all that He has done already, and you will realize that it's only a matter of time before what you are believing for today will come to pass too.

A God Promise

I challenge you, as you read this book, to see God in a light that you may not have seen Him before. See Him as Jehovah Jireh, the Lord God who shall provide. This means that whether it's money, healing, deliverance, salvation or whatever else the need may be, He is faithful to do what He has said He would do.

In closing, I admonish you to be encouraged. While you're waiting on your promise, work in the Kingdom. Do what God has called you to do, and then stand still and see the salvation of the Lord.

God's best blessings be upon you,
Stephanie Johnson, M.Ed.

Introduction

It is my pleasure to share this book with you because it is time for believers to grasp the fact that God is a PROMISE-KEEPER. When He speaks, He speaks to bring awareness, deliverance and so many other blessings to you. But you have to be able to recognize His voice in order to obtain all that He has for you. Knowing when God is speaking will set your life on a course that you would never have imagined before you accepted Christ as your personal Savior. If you have not accepted Christ as your Savior yet, this is the perfect opportunity to do so. Salvation makes you eligible to receive the promises of the Father.

As I write this book, I will speak to you mainly from the second- and third-person point of view. I am intentionally writing in this manner because it is how God instructed me to write. You will see that I refer to you the reader as "you." The second-person point of view is generally only used in instructional writing. It is told from the perspective of "you." The second-person point of view is a form of writing in which the point of view of a narrative work is told in the voice of the "onlooker," which is you, the reader. When I speak to you from this perspective, it is me instructing you on how to proceed to victory. Third-person omniscient is a point of view in which the narrator knows all the thoughts, actions and feelings of all the characters involved. When I speak in this perspective, it is God speaking through me to convey a message to you as the reader and receiver. Therefore, I'm speaking directly to you, as though the Lord Himself is speaking, and this is because He *is*.

You might ask, "Why are you taking the time to explain this?" I'm doing it because I want you, the reader, to understand that when I write, I don't want you to think that I am talking *at* you, and I'm not excluding myself from these lessons. Rather, I want to relay God's message to you in a coherent manner. These lessons are designed as instructional steps to increase your knowledge, wisdom and understanding of the things of God, so that you can apply them in your everyday life.

I will interject PRAISE BREAKS from time to time. These breaks are inserted to instruct you on when it is crucial to give God praise in response to a RHEMA WORD He has spoken. Since we're learning, I believe that these PRAISE BREAKS are a great opportunity to show you how to respond to a word that is "hot off the press" from God. You have to acknowledge that you have heard Him, you honor Him, and you plan to be willing and obedient to respond to Him.

Introduction

It's like saying: "MESSAGE RECEIVED! WILL DO! YES, LORD, I SUBMIT AND I OBEY! YES, LORD, YOU ARE THE POTTER, AND I AM THE CLAY, MAKE ME AND MOLD ME." Do you see? You are to give the appropriate response to whatever God is saying to you in that moment. Seasoned Christians and baby Christians alike will be able to glean from this concept.

Please don't take these breaks for granted; they are for your learning. While I may interject a PRAISE BREAK somewhere in the text where the Lord has spoken to me, I'm sure you will find other places in the text to interject your own praise breaks. When that happens, you are getting it; that is the Word being made alive to you (a *RHEMA WORD*). You will realize that you just received an unction from God, it is happening in real time, and you will know that the *rhema* word is for you.

Last, but not least, I pray that this book brings a newness to you that you have not experienced before. I hope that it unlocks doors and windows that have been shut for a long time because you have not known how to access the blessings behind them. God bless!

Stephanie Johnson
New Orleans, Louisiana

Chapter 1

What Is a Promise?

According to Google Dictionary, the word *promise,* when it is used as a noun, is "a declaration or assurance that one will do a particular thing or that a particular thing will happen." Some synonyms of the word *promise* are "word of honor, word, assurance, pledge, vow, guarantee, oath, bond, undertaking, agreement, commitment, contract, covenant and compact." According to the same dictionary, the word *promise,* when it is used as a verb, means "to assure someone that one will definitely do, give, or arrange something; undertake or declare that something will happen." Synonyms of the word *promise,* when used as a verb, are "swear, pledge, vow, undertake, guarantee, assure, contract, engage, commit oneself, bind oneself, swear/take an oath and make a covenant."

As you can see, *PROMISE* is a power-packed word. If someone promises you something, they have, in essence, made an oath to you that they are bound to fulfill. They must be true to their word. Well, that's what our Lord and Savior has done for us. He has promised, in His Word, that He would never leave us nor forsake us. Because our Father is the True and Living God, when He makes a promise to His people, He does not have to preface it by saying, "Today I promise"; He can just speak the Word, and it will come to pass. Once the Father makes a commitment to us, it is finished. We, as believers, know that God's words will not return to Him void, as it is stated in Isaiah 55:11:

So shall my word be that goeth forth out of my mouth: it shall not return unto me void, but it shall accomplish that which I please, and it shall prosper in the thing whereto I sent it.

When GOD says it, "IT SHALL COME TO PASS," His word will not and cannot bounce back to Him unfulfilled like a boomerang. It shall do what He has commanded it to do. It will happen!

— PRAISE BREAK —
Hallelujah!
What a mighty God we serve!

A simple promise from the Father can turn our entire life around. A mere word from the Lord can open doors, break down walls, release blessings and fill voids in our life. God's Holy Word is a promise to us that He is the Author and the Finisher of our Faith:

Hebrews 12:2

Looking unto Jesus the author and finisher of our faith; who for the joy that was set before him endured the cross, despising the shame, and is set down at the right hand of the throne of God.

He is the Alpha and the Omega:

Revelation 1:8

I am Alpha and Omega, the beginning and the ending, saith the Lord, which is, and which was, and which is to come, the Almighty.

He is the Bright and Morning Star:

Revelation 22:16, NKJV

I, Jesus, have sent My angel to testify to you these things in the churches. I am the Root and the Offspring of David, the Bright and Morning Star.

Most of all, HE IS the Ancient of Days, That, brothers and sisters, means that He has been here forever. There was none before Him, and there will be none after Him. He is the only True and Living God.

Look at what Daniel said as He was seeing a vision from God (AND GET READY FOR ANOTHER PRAISE BREAK)!

Daniel 7:9-10, NKJV

> *I watched till thrones were put in place,*
> *And the Ancient of Days* [this is God the Father]
> *was seated;*
> *His garment was white as snow,*
> *And the hair of His head was like pure wool.*
> *His throne was a fiery flame,*
> *Its wheels a burning fire;*
> *A fiery stream issued*
> *And came forth from before Him.*
> *A thousand thousands ministered to Him;*
> *Ten thousand times ten thousand stood before Him.*
> *The court was seated,*
> *And the books were opened.*

Daniel 7:13-14, NKJV

> *I was watching in the night visions,*
> *And behold, One like the Son of Man* [this is Jesus, the Son],
> *Coming with the clouds of heaven!*
> *He came to the Ancient of Days,*

What Is a Promise?

And they brought Him near before Him [this is the Father and the Son together].
Then to Him was given dominion and glory and a kingdom,
That all peoples, nations, and languages should serve Him.
His dominion is an everlasting dominion,
Which shall not pass away,
And His kingdom the one
Which shall not be destroyed.

— PRAISE BREAK —
Lord, Have Mercy!
This is MIND-BLOWING!

Seeing God the Father and Jesus the Son together in the Word in Daniel's vision just gives me goose bumps. The Father and the Son, two entities, together, with Jesus receiving the honor that is due Him before the actual time has come. In this passage of scripture, God is actually fulfilling HIS PROMISE TO JESUS, HIS SON. He gave Jesus dominion over everything, and we all know that the book of Daniel in the Old Testament comes before the Gospels—Matthew, Mark, Luke and John—which relate stories from Jesus' life on earth. This scripture is a foreshadowing of the fulfilled promise the Father made to Jesus when He said:

A God Promise

Matthew 3:17

> *And lo a voice from heaven, saying,*
> *This is my beloved Son, in whom I am well pleased.*

Oh, clap your hands everybody! Our God is yet on the throne! He is magnificent in His doings! He is worthy to be praised!

Guess what, people of God? I said all of that to say that God is a PROMISE-KEEPER. Now we can begin our journey into *A God Promise*!

Chapter 2

A Promise in Action

Sometimes we, as children of God, tend to read the Word of God and only receive it as valid for the time it was spoken. Child of God, you must learn to apply God's Word for every appropriate situation today. Although the Scriptures were written in certain time periods and addressed to specific characters in specific scenarios, it does not mean that the Word is stagnant or of no effect just because that time has passed. The Scriptures bring life, and God is ever speaking.

There are two ways in which God speaks: the *rhema* word and the *logos* Word. These two words—*rhema* and *logos*—are both derived from the Greek and refer to the Word of God. *Rhema* is the spoken word of God.

According to *The Advanced Training Institute International*, the second primary Greek word that describes Scripture is *rhema*, which refers to a word that is spoken and means "an utterance." A *rhema* is a verse or portion of scripture that the Holy Spirit brings to our attention with application to a current situation or need for direction.

Receiving a *rhema* word is like a death row inmate receiving a stay of execution just in the nick of time. It is a word that brings life and a solution to a problem, not to mention many other results.

In short, a *rhema* word is a real-time word of knowledge or word of wisdom that comes to bring you answers to your current questions, to bring peace to your soul and to bring light into your darkness. When you receive a *rhema* word, take heed to it because God has shown you that He loves you enough to speak to you directly in this day and time.

Many people do not believe that God still speaks in the twenty-first century, not to mention that His Word comes off of the pages of the Bible, to heal, minister and deliver, but it does. You are so precious to God that He said in His Word:

Psalm 8:4-6

> *What is man, that thou art mindful of him? and the son of man, that thou visitest him? For thou hast made him a little lower than the angels, and hast crowned him with glory and honour. Thou madest him to have dominion over the works of thy hands; thou hast put all things under his feet.*

David was posing a rhetorical question as he praised the Lord. He already understood God's love toward us. He knew that God had such a tremendous passion for us, as His children, that He would consider our thoughts, feelings, pains and struggles, etc. He knew that God actually tended to us as we journeyed through this world. David was in awe of God. He admired Him so much that he wanted to kiss God with his words of admiration and appreciation.

— PRAISE BREAK —
To Him who sits on the throne be glory and honor and power forever!

As a believer, you must know that the Bible states, in Paul's second letter to Timothy, that every word of it is inspired by God:

2 Timothy 3:16
> *All scripture is given by inspiration of God, and is profitable for doctrine, for reproof, for correction, for instruction in righteousness.*

It also states in Matthew 4:

Matthew 4:4
> *Man shall not live by bread alone, but by every word* [rhema] *that proceedeth out of the mouth of God.*

Last, but certainly not least, Jesus also stated:

A God Promise

John 6:63

> *The words* [rhema] *that I speak unto you, they are spirit, and they are life.*

Many times, when a *rhema* word is given by God, it may confirm His Word by giving a second *rhema* word, as stated in the Scriptures:

2 Corinthians 13:1

> *In the mouth of two or three witnesses shall every word* [rhema] *be established.*

Well, that was a lot said in a few pages. In essence, a *rhema* word is what every believer needs to survive the journey we have been called to travel. Although the Word of God is alive as it is written, you cannot possibly survive unless that Word jumps off the page at you, and you can then apply it to your daily life. When this happens, you are actually experiencing in real time what Jesus said in John 14:26:

> *But the Comforter, which is the Holy Ghost, whom the Father will send in my name, he shall teach you all things, and bring all things to your remembrance, whatsoever I have said unto you.*

Just for clarification, when I say "real time," I mean that you're receiving a word as though it is happening right at that very moment. When Jesus left the earth, He said He would send the Comforter to be with us, and He did. He sent God, the Holy Spirit. The Holy Spirit's job on this earth is to dwell in you, guide you, empower you, equip you and so much more ... if you allow Him to do it. He does His job by speaking the Word, just as Jesus and the Father did because they are one. Although you have seen them in different roles and manifestations throughout the Scriptures, God the Father, Jesus the Son and the Holy Spirit ARE INDEED ONE!

One of the Holy Spirit's primary jobs is to bring the Word alive to you. As the Holy Spirit performs that duty, Jesus Christ the Righteous sits at the right hand of the Father, praying for you, that you do not fail. As the Holy Spirit and Jesus are fulfilling their purpose, the Father watches over His Word to perform it.

Excuse me while I interject another PRAISE BREAK right here. Did you just see the omnipotent, omniscient, sovereign workings of God (Father, Son and Holy Spirit) right there? The Divine Trinity—Father God, the Holy Spirit and Jesus the Christ are so intertwined, interconnected, and interdependent that THEY CANNOT BE SEPARATED! Hallelujah! Praise His name!

— PRAISE BREAK —
EXALT HIM!
MAGNIFY HIM!
HONOR HIM!

A God Promise

Go ahead! Just go ahead and give Him praise right now! Yes, He is worthy.

Life Lesson Learned: You know the "*rhema* word" of God is real, and it is how God speaks to us today in real time. When you pray daily, you are asking God for a right-now word, a word in season, a word of deliverance, a word of wisdom or word of knowledge. You are asking God for a personalized promise, a promise just for you. His Word applied to your life will meet your needs and guide you on your journey.

Learn to allow the Holy Spirit to speak to you in the only way He will, and that is through the Scriptures. Let the Word of God come alive in your life and hold on to the promises He gives you to overcome each and every challenge in your life.

When you hear God speak, respond and keep the communication going. As you present yourself before God, He will come in and live with you. Sit in His presence and wait for His manifestation. He manifests Himself with a word, a song or a vision.

No matter how God chooses to manifest, you must respond to His presence. 1). First, acknowledge that you know He is present. 2). Second, reverence Him by giving Him praise. 3). Third, respond to what He has said, whether it is a simple, "Yes, Lord," or you begin to make your requests known to Him.

In several scriptures, the Bible uses the word *intreat* (modern, *entreat*). For instance, *"Intreat the LORD"* (Exodus

A Promise in Action

9:28). According to *Webster's Dictionary*, *entreat* means "to plead with, especially in order to persuade: ask urgently." When you commune with the Father, it is not only Him speaking to you, but you speaking back to Him. Oh, and did I mention what I call "the listening factor." Listening for God's voice is crucial. You must make sure that your spirit is open to hear what God is saying. This thought is written several times in the Bible so that you can understand how important it is to hear God:

Matthew 11:15

He that hath ears to hear, let him hear.

Revelation 2:7

He that hath an ear, let him hear what the Spirit saith unto the churches.

Revelation 10:17

So then faith cometh by hearing, and hearing by the word of God.

Over and over again, we are admonished to "hear." This is not only an individual hearing, but, as the Bride of Christ, the Church is also mandated to hear what the Spirit is saying.

Don't misunderstand me. God can speak to anyone when He wants to, and they will hear, and they will listen, if God has ordained it to be so; but the purpose here is to cultivate a life wherein you can hear God regularly when He speaks. Establishing a consistent two-way communication with God is what's needed to ensure that you are walking in destiny and purpose. Ultimately, receiving a *rhema* word from God, requires that you are open to hearing God and that you then respond to Him.

Chapter 3

Logos, the Power of the Written Word!

After that exhaustive lesson on the *rhema* word of God, now we need to examine the *Logos Word*. Like the *rhema* word, the *Logos* Word is also scripture. It is the written Word of God. It is the record that we have from the time of the original writings God inspired.

According to *Advanced Training Institute International*, *logos* refers principally to "the total inspired Word of God and to Jesus, Who is the living Logos." I see the *Logos* Word as our point of reference. It is like the articles of faith that you might have in a legal document of a religious organization, and that organization is bound by those articles. The articles are instituted to hold the participants of the organizations accountable, to maintain a certain standard in their faith. After all, in essence, they are the established doctrine on how to conduct oneself in the business of the organization or church. The *Logos* Word is what we, as Christians, live by and what we communicate to others as our standard for living.

In today's society, there is a philosophy or way of thinking that is being called "your truth," but it is dubbed "the truth." I will later discuss this new phenomenon "speak your truth" that has emerged over the last few years. The *Logos* Word is the foundation for a Christian's success. For a sinner, it is the pathway to righteousness. Here is some evidence for these facts:

Psalm 119:11

Thy word [logos] *have I hid in mine heart, that I might not sin against thee.*

Psalm 119:105

Thy word [logos] *is a lamp unto my feet, and a light unto my path.*

John 1:1

In the beginning was the Word [logos], *and the Word* [logos] *was with God, and the Word* [logos] *was God.*

2 Timothy 2:15

Study to show thyself approved unto God, a workman that needeth not to be ashamed, rightly dividing the word [logos] *of truth.*

Logos, the Power of the Written Word!

Hebrews 4:12

> *For the word* [logos] *of God is quick, and powerful.*

1 Peter 1:23

> *Being born again, not of corruptible seed, but of incorruptible, by the word* [logos] *of God, which liveth and abideth forever.*

The Bible is defined as the Christian Scriptures, consisting of the sixty-six books of the Old and New Testaments. Wikipedia states that the word *Bible* comes from the Koine Greek, meaning "the books." It is a collection of sacred texts or scriptures that Jews and Christians consider to be a product of divine inspiration and a record of the relationship between God and humans.

Many different authors contributed to the Bible. What is now regarded as canonical text differs depending on traditions and groups. Note: *canonical* is defined as "included in the list of sacred books officially accepted as genuine."

The *Logos* Word provides the written account of the happenings in the world, as historians know it, from the beginning of time until the writing of the last book of the Bible. It is the God-inspired writing that allows man to become acquainted with the history of God's dealings with mankind.

We know that God created everything in the beginning, as we see in John 1:3:

A God Promise

John 1:3

All things were made by him; and without him was not any thing made that was made.

This is the evidence that the Word of God was here in the beginning, and Jesus is the Word of God. God manifested His living Word in a written format.

Now, back to that new phrase, "my truth." You have, no doubt, heard the saying "speak your truth" or "I'm speaking my truth." It's all over the TV networks and social media, and it's in our communities and churches, but I have to tell you that "*your* truth" is not always "*the* truth." That's the danger of this modern message. Many people are "speaking *their* truth" because it is said that this will liberate them or justify their behavior or what they have been through, but the real truth is: no matter what you've been through or how you feel, there is only one truth, and that is the truth according to God's Word.

This would not be such a sensitive area if it were not for the fact of how this "statement" is being used across America and the world. The devil is using it to deceive thousands of people into believing that whatever they say or claim is true is actually true. The Bible says, *"Let God be true but every man a liar"* (Romans 3:4, NKJV).

"Why is this so dangerous?" you might ask. "People are simply expressing themselves and what they feel." My brothers and sisters, the danger of it is that if the enemy can deceive you by making you believe that "it is what it is," then he can destroy you. You have to remember that the enemy is an evil force in the earth, and his total agenda is to steal from you, kill you and destroy you, your family and everything you hold dear. It is his job to interject new deceptions on a regular basis into the land so that the people of God will let down their guard and believe a lie, and, ultimately, the promises of God will have no effect in their lives. If the enemy can get you to believe a lie, you CANNOT hold on to the promises of God.

God's promises are *"YEA"* AND *"AMEN!"* (2 Corinthians 1:20). "Speaking *your* truth" allows anyone and everyone to determine what is right in their own eyes. In other words, there are no boundaries. There is no good or evil. There is no right or wrong. But the Bible warns us in Proverbs 14:

Proverbs 14:12, NKJV

> *There is a way that seems right to a man,*
> *But its end is the way of death.*

In other words, beware of living your life based upon every new word that arrives on the scene. Focus your eyes and heart on what God is saying, and remember: the principles you live by should be based on the Word of God. When you face challenges in life that are too difficult to bear and you feel condemned by the situation, give it to Jesus. Stand on the promises of God, this one in particular:

A God Promise

Hebrews 4:15

For we have not an high priest which cannot be touched with the feeling of our infirmities; but was in all points tempted like as we are, yet without sin.

Jesus took our sin upon Himself that He might fulfill His promise to the Father. He did not change God's plan by "speaking His own truth." Jesus' truth was and is the Father's truth, that He was predestined to die on the cross and rise again to redeem mankind back to God the Father.

Jesus could have chosen to have His own truth, which could have been used when He was in the Garden of Gethsemane and prayed, *"Let this cup pass from me."* What if Jesus had said to the Father in that moment, "My truth is that I don't want to go to the cross, and so I'm not going. I don't want to do this?" Where would we be? The entire plan of God would have been sabotaged by one thought during a time of weakness. Praise be to God that Jesus' thoughts had to be subject to the plan and the purpose of God the Father for His life. Jesus obeyed the Father until the very end.

— PRAISE BREAK —
**Glory to God in the highest!
Thank You, Jesus, for fulfilling
Your purpose on Earth.**

Logos, the Power of the Written Word!

Although that one peek into scripture allows us to see Jesus' humanity, it was not there to give us an "out" in order to do what we feel like doing. Rather, it is there to let us know that we will get weak, and we will fall short, but by keeping sight of the promises of God, we can prevail. Read the story so that you will see the importance of coming through a trial and staying focused on the promise, no matter what you may have to endure:

Matthew 26:36-42

Then cometh Jesus with them unto a place called Gethsemane, and saith unto the disciples, Sit ye here, while I go and pray yonder. And he took with him Peter and the two sons of Zebedee, and began to be sorrowful and very heavy. Then saith he unto them, My soul is exceeding sorrowful, even unto death: tarry ye here, and watch with me.

And he went a little farther, and fell on his face, and prayed, saying, O my Father, if it be possible, let this cup pass from me: nevertheless not as I will, but as thou wilt.

And he cometh unto the disciples, and findeth them asleep, and saith unto Peter, What, could ye not watch with me one hour? Watch and pray, that ye enter not into temptation: the spirit indeed is willing, but the flesh is weak.

A God Promise

He went away again the second time, and prayed, saying, O my Father, if this cup may not pass away from me, except I drink it, thy will be done.

As Jesus pointed out, His spirit was willing, but His flesh was weak. And this, my friends, is how the enemy brings in deception. He does it during our times of weakness. Instead of overcoming the trial, we tend to give in, and when we give in, we justify our actions by calling it "our truth." We change what we know is wrong into something right because we can't overcome the temptation and because we are not holding on to the promise of God. If you want to overcome a negative situation in your life that you know is not of God and you have been justifying it by calling it "your truth," pray this prayer with me:

Father, in the name of Jesus, I denounce the deceptions of Satan, and I believe that You are my Deliverer. I come boldly to the throne of grace to find help in the time of need. I will no longer justify my sins, but I place them on the altar. Forgive me, and deliver me, Lord. Wash me in Your blood. I believe Your Word is true. Thank You for deliverance.

In Jesus' name,
Amen!

Chapter 4

Is it God or the Devil?

The big question that many people ask, when coming to the knowledge of the truth that God is alive and does actually speak, is this: How do you know it's God speaking and not the devil? Well, that's a loaded question, but I seem to recall that when I accepted Christ more than thirty years ago, I asked that same question. How do you know? What are the signs that distinguish God's voice from the enemy's voice? How can you tell you're not imagining what you're hearing?

I'm sure that the Lord had spoken to me many times before I actually came to the realization that He was the one speaking to me. Looking back, I'm certain that He spoke to me on many occasions when I thought "something said" or "something told me," and that "something" prevented problems or gave me wisdom in the midst of situations I didn't know how to handle. Eventually I realized that the "something" was God. It was not just a chance feeling or thought, but it was God speaking to me, although He had not allowed me to recognize Him yet. After I became a Christian, it was like blinders had been removed from my eyes, and I began to realize that I was no longer only a part of a natural world, but that the spiritual word was also very real.

Because I was a babe in Christ, it was important that I discovered the truth about how and when God speaks. I wanted to know how to distinguish God's voice from all others. In search of answers on how to know that God is speaking, I began reading His Word. I wanted to know when He was speaking so that I could be obedient to His voice. I wanted to know how to access His promises.

In the beginning, I didn't know much about God, but it was my desire to learn all that I could. I knew one thing for sure: that it was God who had delivered me from my nightmares, fears and foolishness. I knew that it was God who had manifested Himself in a dream at the point of my desperation and rescued me. I knew it was God who had led me to church one Resurrection morning more than thirty years ago, and I wept throughout the entire sermon. It was God Who motivated me to go to the altar, where I lifted my hands into the air (with no one directing me to do so), as a sign of my surrender to Him. What I'm saying is this: God was speaking to me the entire time. He was leading me and ministering to me through dreams, things that were happening in my life and my friends. His Word had come into my life to draw me, and I hadn't even realized what was happening until it was done.

When I reflect on this now, I can clearly see that God drew me just as Jeremiah 31:3 states:

> *The LORD hath appeared of old unto me, saying, Yea, I have loved thee with an everlasting love: therefore, with lovingkindness have I drawn thee.*

No man can tell God when to initiate His pursuit of your soul back to Him. God decides how to speak to you and when to speak to you, and He uses different methods for different people. It is all founded upon His Word. Just as in the story of Balaam and his dubm ass in Numbers 22:

Numbers 22:28
> *And the LORD opened the mouth of the ass, and she said unto Balaam, What have I done unto thee, that thou hast smitten me these three times?*

God allowed a donkey to speak to Balaam in order to save his life. You should read the entire story.

God spoke in 1 Kings 19:

1 Kings 19:11-12
> *And he said, Go forth, and stand upon the mount before the LORD. And, behold, the LORD passed by, and a great*

and strong wind rent the mountains, and brake in pieces the rocks before the LORD; but the LORD was not in the wind: and after the wind an earthquake; but the LORD was not in the earthquake: and after the earthquake a fire; but the LORD was not in the fire: and after the fire a still small voice.

God was not in the noise. We often think of Him as a roaring, loud God, but He can also speak in a still small voice. He can manifest Himself however He chooses. You need to be open to hear and watch for His manifestation.

He spoke to Moses through a burning bush:

Exodus 3:2-5

And the angel of the LORD appeared unto him in a flame of fire out of the midst of a bush: and he looked, and, behold, the bush burned with fire, and the bush was not consumed. And Moses said, I will now turn aside, and see this great sight, why the bush is not burnt.

And when the LORD saw that he turned aside to see, God called unto him out of the midst of the bush, and said, Moses, Moses.

And he said, Here am I.

And he said, Draw not nigh hither: put off thy shoes from off thy feet, for the place whereon thou standest is holy ground.

Is it God or the Devil?

God is creative in His manner of speaking to us. He manifests in such a way that we know it could only be Him. The point is: God can choose anyone, anything or any circumstance to speak to you.

Now, let's get back to whether it is God speaking or the devil speaking. The Bible says:

John 10:4-5

And when he putteth forth his own sheep, he goeth before them, and the sheep follow him: for they know his voice. And a stranger will they not follow, but will flee from him: for they know not the voice of strangers.

God's Word has clear characteristics that reveal that it is indeed Him speaking. Please take note here, when God speaks, the following will be present:

- What He speaks will be aligned with and consistent with His written Word.
- What He speaks will not support carnality or worldliness.
- What He speaks will lead you further into the truth and into a God-kind of life.
- What He speaks will challenge you to live by faith and increase in the Word.
- What He speaks may require you to do things that seem hard and beyond your capabilities, but through

faith and development in the Word, He will enable You to do what He has said, so that you might grow in Him.

- What He speaks will edify you.
- What He speaks will clearly reveal His will to you.

These are, by no means, all of the characteristics of God's speaking, but they are certainly a good start and will help you understand His voice. As you read the Bible and pray, God will enlighten you and show you more.

If God's Word is a lamp and a light, you cannot walk in deception because He is guiding you. You have to trust His Word to lead you and guide you into all truth.

Regarding the characteristics of when the enemy is speaking, there is a clear distinction. The enemy's ways are contrary to God's ways. Therefore, his actions, his voice and his plan are in direct rebellion to the things of God. You will know when the enemy is speaking if you pay attention to what the outcome of what he says will be. Will what is being said cause you to disobey God's Word? Will it bring separation from the things of God? The Bible states that you should:

1 Peter 5:8-9

Be sober, be vigilant; because your adversary the devil, as a roaring lion, walketh about, seeking whom he may devour: whom resist stedfast in the faith, knowing that the same afflictions are accomplished in your brethren that are in the world.

The Bible also instructs you to:

James 4:7

Submit yourselves therefore to God. Resist the devil, and he will flee from you.

God gives you a wealth of information on how to be victorious over the wiles of the enemy. All you have to do is take heed.

— PRAISE BREAK —
Thank God for salvation!

Will overcoming the enemy be easy? NO! Will you always be able to see clearly? NO! You must pray and ask God for wisdom. His Word assures you that if you ask Him for wisdom, He will freely give it to you. Child of God, you can do this. While all of this may seem to be a lot and quite overwhelming, God has equipped you with everything you need to succeed. You can *"do all things through Christ which strengtheneth"* you (Philippians 4:13).

Here are some signs that the enemy is speaking:

- Because he is a liar and a deceiver, he will distort God's Word in order to deceive you. When he speaks, his conversation has an underlying tone of rebellion to God's will. He challenges you to do things yourself and not wait on God.

- He accuses God when he speaks. (Why hasn't God healed you? Why didn't God protect you? etc.).

- Old Slewfoot is referred to in John 10:10 as *"the thief"*: *"The thief cometh not, but for to steal, and to kill, and to destroy: I [Jesus] am come that they might have life, and that they might have it more abundantly."* Therefore, whenever the enemy is speaking to you, his entire focus is on stealing what God has given you. He does not want you to receive the blessings or the promises of God.

- He comes to tempt you the same way he did Jesus in the wilderness. With Jesus, he used the lust of the flesh, the lust of the eyes and the pride of life. When he speaks, he is constantly trying to offer you something that he really does not have to give. His goal is to find your weakness and to seduce you into turning away from God.

Satan is a trickster. He twists and distorts things to make them appear real or "like truth" in order to deceive you. I mentioned earlier the new phrase that is making the rounds—"my truth." What the enemy has done is to make people think that as long it is true to *them*, then it's okay. It doesn't matter what the Bible says or what is truly right, as long as it is right to *you*. If it is "your truth," then it's all good. This concept is directly from the pit of Hell. It is a strong delusion, developed by Satan himself to lure millions of people into death, Hell and destruction.

Again, there is no such thing as "*your* truth"; there is "*the* truth," and this is what is rooted and grounded in the Word of God. The enemy has propped up many of today's greatest deceptions upon this concept, "live your truth," but it is a lie. Consequently, many people today are doing exactly what was done in Judges 17:6:

> *In those days there was no king in Israel, but every man did that which was right in his own eyes.*

People are living their lives according to what *they think* is right, with no point of reference for the real truth. As long as it sounds good, makes you feel good and works with your lifestyle, it's all good ... or so they think. How foolish! The Bible says that Satan is *"the father"* of lies:

John 8:44

> *Ye are of your father the devil, and the lusts of your father ye will do. He was a murderer from the beginning, and abode not in the truth, because there is no truth in him. When he speaketh a lie, he speaketh of his own: for he is a liar, and the father of it.*

A God Promise

Just as I mentioned concerning the characteristics of when God is speaking, there are certainly more ways that the enemy can speak to you. Therefore, it is incumbent upon you to seek God to understand how to resist the enemy in every situation.

In these last days, like never before, the Church will be confronted with "new" social norms that are seemingly acceptable and good. However, they will surely be directly inspired and orchestrated by Satan to get the Church on a downward spiral away from God and to encourage us to abandon the promises of God. To protect yourself, hide these scriptures in your heart:

1 Peter 4:18-19

> *And if the righteous scarcely be saved, where shall the ungodly and the sinner appear? Wherefore let them that suffer according to the will of God commit the keeping of their souls to him in well doing, as unto a faithful Creator.*

2 Thessalonians 2:2-3

> *That ye be not soon shaken in mind, or be troubled, neither by spirit, nor by word, nor by letter as from us, as that the day of Christ is at hand. Let no man deceive you by any means: for that day shall not come, except there come a falling away first, and that man of sin be revealed, the son of perdition.*

Is it God or the Devil?

Saints of God, I cannot overemphasize how critical it is that you are able to recognize and hear God's voice in these last days. Your very life depends on it. However, let me say there is no hysteria here, only great caution. When you know that you know God and His voice, you are safe in His arms. He gives you peace that passes all understanding. The thing is: you must get to know Him, for you don't want to be one of those who falls away.

One of God's most well-known promises is given in John 3:16:

> For God so loved the world, that He gave His only begotten Son, that whoever believes in Him should not perish but have everlasting life. (NKJV)

You, too, can live eternally with God.

Chapter 5

A God Promise

One day, as I was going about my regular routine, the Lord began to speak to me about the fact that when He makes a promise, you can rest assured that it will come to pass. This reminded me of my mom sitting us children down to talk to us and "school" us on different things we needed to know. These were always messages for our good. That day the Father began to "school" me on how important it is to be aligned with His will because He knows the desires of our hearts. After all, He put them there. When you're believing God to walk in your destiny, you have to remember: your destiny is in God's hands, and in order to realize that destiny, you have to be a GOD-SEEKER.

As the "schooling" went on, the Lord showed me that we all have such desires for our life, and we think we have a pretty good idea of how they will manifest, but then He reminded me of His Word in Isaiah 55:8-9:

A God Promise

For my thoughts are not your thoughts, neither are your ways my ways, saith the LORD. For as the heavens are higher than the earth, so are my ways higher than your ways, and my thoughts than your thoughts.

He is saying to us today: "You think you have it all figured out, but I have an even better way that will totally blow your mind. My plans will trump your plans any day of the week because I am God." His Word declares:

Jeremiah 29:11

For I know the thoughts that I think toward you, saith the LORD, thoughts of peace, and not of evil, to give you an expected end.

The New Testament records:

1 Corinthians 2:9

But as it is written, Eye hath not seen, nor ear heard, neither have entered into the heart of man, the things which God hath prepared for them that love him.

Saints, you might ask, "Well, then, how do you know it's God speaking to you?" I know because He uses His Word to speak. When you stop to listen to God, He will bring back the Word that you have read in times past to minister to you.

A God Promise

During this "schooling," it was as if the Lord was showing me, "Stephanie, I love you so much. You can't even fathom what I have on the horizon for you. What you think is a blessing can't compare to what I have planned because you are My own. When I make a promise, it is '*A God Promise*,' a promise that cannot be broken."

Another dictionary, *Merriam Webster's,* defines *promise* as "A. a declaration that one will do or refrain from doing something specific, and B. a legally binding declaration that gives the person to whom it is made a right to expect or to claim the performance or forbearance of a specified act." The Online Dictionary gives the following synonyms for the word *promise*: "assurance, pledge, vow, guarantee, oath, bond, undertaking, agreement, commitment, contract, covenant." Wow! I love that! When the Father makes a promise, He does it to assure you that He will perform His Word. Not only that; He is so confident in His Word and in Himself, because He is God, that He allows you to expect the promise to be fulfilled.

You have every right to expect God's promise to come to pass. Let me say that again. As a child of God, you have a right to expect God's promises to manifest in your life:

Hebrews 6:13
> *For when God made promise to Abraham, because he could swear by no greater, he swore by himself.*

A God Promise

As noted, Hebrews 6:13 confirms that His promises are *"YEA"* and *"AMEN."* In a nutshell, this means that His Word is true, and it shall be done. *Amen* denotes "so be it" or "it is finished." My God is awesome. Now that merits a praise break. Give Him your own words of praise.

— PRAISE BREAK —

Now that we have settled the fact that God cannot break His promises and that His promises are far greater than what we can imagine, let's discuss how to activate God's promises in your life. First and foremost, let me offer this disclaimer: there is no one way, no cookie-cutter pattern in which God moves for every person. However, He does set the criteria in His Word for His children receiving blessings through that Word.

Before you ask, "CRITERIA?" let me explain. Yes, God freely gives salvation to all who accept, plus many other benefits from just knowing and walking with Him. However, there are some promises that are hinged upon your willingness and obedience as His child. He spoke to His people in the book of Isaiah, warning against rebelling against Him and walking in disobedience:

Isaiah 1:18-20

Come now, and let us reason together, saith the LORD: though your sins be as scarlet, they shall be as white as snow; though they be red like crimson, they shall be as wool. If ye be willing and obedient, ye shall eat the good of the land: but if ye refuse and rebel, ye shall be devoured with the sword: for the mouth of the LORD hath spoken it.

This passage of scripture clearly indicates that God is displeased with sin and disobedience. His entire discourse in this passage was a plea to convince the people to turn back to Him. It is not His will that even one of His people perish, but He will not lower His standards for anyone. It is our responsibility to allow God to change us from the inside out. We have to acknowledge that He is the Potter, and we are the clay. We have to surrender our lives to Him in order to walk in His promises, laying aside every weight and the sin that challenges us.

Although God has made His sun to shine on the just and the unjust and His rain to do the same, we should never take His love and mercy for granted. He does these things because He is a merciful God. These blessings are because of His undying love for us. You must get to a place where you can receive His blessings because of the covenant relationship you have with Him and not just because of His mercy.

Child of God, you must declare war on the things that tend to separate you from the will of God. If you want God, you have to make this known to Him—even though He already knows your heart. You have to verbalize to Him your desire to serve Him. Whether it is at home and you are all alone or in a crowded church with a bunch of strangers, you must express from your heart your need for God. Yes, I'm talking about accepting Him as your Lord and Savior.

Repentance is absolutely the first step in activating His promises. Take a look at this passage from Romans 10:

Romans 10:9-11

> *That if thou shalt confess with thy mouth the Lord Jesus, and shalt believe in thine heart that God hath raised him from the dead, thou shalt be saved. For with the heart man believeth unto righteousness; and with the mouth confession is made unto salvation. For the scripture saith, Whosoever believeth on him shall not be ashamed.*

In Psalm 51, David offered a prayer of repentance to God after having a visit from a prophet named Nathan. In essence, Nathan told David that his family would be cursed with death and destruction because he had killed Uriah, the husband of Bathsheba, so that he could have her. When David prayed, he made a powerful statement:

Psalm 51:5

> *Behold, I was shapen in iniquity; and in sin did my mother conceive me.*

I submit to you that if David was formed and created in iniquity, all of us were too, for all men were created equally.

A God Promise

After the fall of Adam and Eve, sin passed upon all men. Sin was in our bloodline, even as an infant. Until we HAVE BEEN REDEEMED BACK TO GOD and come to the knowledge of Jesus Christ, we CANNOT WALK IN HIS PROMISES! In order to activate these promises, you must have an understanding of what is required, so that you can walk in your rightful place as an heir of Christ.

After you have accepted God's will for your life, you need to be taught how to be a good steward of His Word. Hence, this second step is so that God can show you through His Word how to inherit His promises. We are admonished in 2 Timothy 2:15:

> *Study to shew thyself approved unto God, a workman that needeth not to be ashamed, rightly dividing the word of truth.*

If you want God's validation, you have to understand who God is and how He operates. You have to study His Word (the Bible) so that you can understand how you should live as an heir of Christ.

Let me stop right here. I am *not* saying that God is a God who requires *works* for salvation. What I am saying is that the Lord validates His people when they are willing and obedient. You can be saved and live like you are, just another person with no benefits. If you choose, you can have a surface relationship with God. His desire, however, is that you go deeper into His truths. In order for that to happen, you must seek Him by learning His Word.

In God's Word is where you will find His promises. These promises are made available to you if you want them. The Scriptures tell us: *"work out your own salvation"* (Philippians 2:12). This means to become disciplined and well-groomed in the Word of God.

Romans 12 offers some examples of what it looks like to be a good steward of God's Word:

Romans 12:10-18

> *Be kindly affectioned one to another with brotherly love; in honor preferring one another; not slothful in business; fervent in spirit; serving the Lord; rejoicing in hope; patient in tribulation; continuing instant in prayer; distributing to the necessity of saints; given to hospitality.*
>
> *Bless them which persecute you: bless, and curse not. Rejoice with them that do rejoice, and weep with them that weep. Be of the same mind one toward another. Mind not high things, but condescend to men of low estate. Be not wise in your own conceits. Recompense to no man evil for evil. Provide things honest in the sight of all men. If it be possible, as much as lieth in you, live peaceably with all men.*

A God Promise

These scriptures represent just a hint of the wisdom that God has provided for us to live by.

When you are a child of God, you innately seek truth, knowledge and understanding. The Holy Spirit (who dwells in you) causes you to desire more of God, and you truly want to live holy in God's sight. When you crave His Word, you are actually being transformed according to that Word:

Romans 12:1-2

> *I beseech you therefore, brethren, by the mercies of God, that ye present your bodies a living sacrifice, holy, acceptable unto God, which is your reasonable service. And be not conformed to this world: but be ye transformed by the renewing of your mind, that ye may prove what is that good, and acceptable, and perfect, will of God.*

"A God Promise" is all-encompassing. It includes the Father making and keeping His promises, but it also includes the child of God being willing and obedient, being a good steward, being able to understand the *rhema* and the *Logos* Word for daily living. We tend to think that God's promises are one-sided, but in order for you to be a recipient of His promises, which exceed what I call "regular or normal grace," you must put yourself in a position as a candidate for those blessings.

A God Promise

Allow me to reiterate: you qualify for God's love just because of who He is. You cannot earn His love. You cannot work for His grace, mercy or favor. With that said, please remember these words: *grace, mercy* and *favor*. Here are the definitions according to *Miriam Webster's Dictionary:*

- *Favor*—"an act of kindness beyond what is due or usual"
- *Mercy*—"compassion or forbearance shown especially to an offender or to one subject to one's power; also lenient or compassionate treatment"
- *Grace*—"unmerited divine assistance given humans for their regeneration or sanctification, a virtue coming from God, a state of sanctification enjoyed through divine assistance" In the church, *grace* is well known as "God's unmerited favor."

It is important that you understand that all of the aforementioned words denote a gift presented that has not been earned. It also does not mandate any form of repayment, negotiation or sacrifice. It is freely given because of the giver's desire. The Father has plans for a blessed future for His children.

Going beyond just attending church on Sundays indicates that you are ready to enter into another realm of knowing God. Because He is omnipotent (all powerful), omnipresent (present everywhere at the same time) and omniscient (all knowing), how can we neglect so great a salvation? My sentiments resonate with David's when he wrote Psalm 139:

Psalm 139:7-12

> *Whither shall I go from thy spirit? or whither shall I flee from thy presence? If I ascend up into heaven, thou art there: if I make my bed in hell, behold, thou art there. If I take the wings of the morning, and dwell in the uttermost parts of the sea; even there shall thy hand lead me, and thy right hand shall hold me. If I say, Surely the darkness shall cover me; even the night shall be light about me. Yea, the darkness hideth not from thee; but the night shineth as the day: the darkness and the light are both alike to thee.*

OH, MY! God's Word is so very powerful. Even as I write these words to you, I feel the awesomeness of His power. Hallelujah! Great God!

The one thing I want to leave with you about *A God Promise* is that God *will be* who He is, but will you be who He wants you to be?

The heavenly Father validated Jesus after He had been baptized by John in the Jordan River. By speaking in an audible voice, the Father acknowledged that He was pleased with His Son.

A God Promise

The more you develop a relationship with the Father, the more His Word will come alive to you as a *rhema* word of life, and you will be able to learn how to walk in God's divine blessings for your everyday life.

Chapter 6

Obtaining the Promise

Becoming who God wants you to be requires a lot of soul searching.

— PRAISE BREAK —
Just stop right here and give God a hand of praise
for His great wisdom!

As we entered into 2019, the Holy Spirit revealed to me that I had to get downright angry enough to declare war on some of the things in my life that were not up to par. It was not good enough to *want* things to change, or even to *pray* that they change. I had to *make* them change.

"And how do you do that?" you might ask. Well, the first thing is to stop whining and complaining and feeling sorry for yourself about what's not working or what's not right in your life. We (church people included) spend far too much time focusing on the negative. If we could contain the tears that we have shed as a representation of how much we pity ourselves and our conditions, we probably could fill every body of water in the country collectively. You know I'm right.

When things aren't going well, before we can kick into gear to make some changes, we automatically seem to kick into a feel-sorry-for-myself mode. Sometimes we go through days, weeks and even months of self-pity, crying about what's wrong: Why me? Why won't anyone help me? etc. We go through a litany of reasons for why we just can't make it. We just can't help it. We just can't change it. It's too hard. It costs too much. It's going to take too long. This doesn't end until one day we get a revelation that we're in control of the situation—if we would just step up and attack the matter with the Word. That Word declares:

Psalm 18:29

For by thee I have run through a troop; and by my God have I leaped over a wall.

All the while, God is standing there beckoning us to come into the fullness of His presence, and many times we can't get past whatever happened—bad credit, loss of a friendship, divorce, sickness in the family or other life issues. Jesus said:

Obtaining the Promise

Revelation 3:20-21

> *Behold, I stand at the door, and knock: if any man hear my voice, and open the door, I will come in to him, and will sup with him, and he with me. To him that overcometh will I grant to sit with me in my throne, even as I also overcame, and am set down with my Father in his throne.*

Instead of heeding and opening the door to our Deliverer, we tend to dwell on the loss we have suffered, how it happened and when it happened and all of the rest of the drama. We should keep our eyes on Christ, knowing that He is the Alpha and Omega.

As Paul wrote to the Philippian believers:

Philippians 1:6, NKJV

> *Being confident of this very thing, that He who has begun a good work in you will complete it until the day of Jesus Christ.*

Let's make this declaration together, right now! Repeat after me:

AIN'T NO SENSE IN CRYING!
DECLARE WAR!
OBTAIN THE PROMISE!

A God Promise

Declare war on who? Declare war on the situation, the devil and your flesh! You have to get tired of being defeated in small things so that you can be victorious in the bigger things.

Jeremiah 12:5, NKJV

If you have run with the footmen, and they have wearied you,
Then how can you contend with horses?

If you cannot overcome the little day-to-day aggravations of life, how can you master the real challenges? 2 Corinthians 12:7-10 tells us, for example, that demons and imps are assigned to our life to hinder us and to keep us from becoming prideful, believing we no longer need God. Paul called this a *"thorn in the flesh"* (verse 7). Like him, you might even pray over and over again for something to be removed, and, instead, the Lord will tell you that His grace is sufficient for you to deal with the situation. He assures you that His strength is made perfect in your weakness. Then you will realize that when you are weak you are indeed strong.

We would all like to think we have it "going on," but the truth is that we all have struggles. At some point in our lives, the answer is learning how to go through it and come out of it in one piece and victorious. I'm realizing that no matter how old I am in the Lord, I'm learning something new every day. I guess it depends on what you're going through at the moment. You have a bank of scriptures stored up in you from years of walking with God, but until you go through a situation that brings a certain scripture to the forefront, you don't really understand how that scripture applies to your personal life. In the trial, it becomes more real than ever before, and once again you realize how awesome God is and how His promises stand, no matter what's happening in your isolated condition. It's at these times when you may find yourself in a daily battle to keep your mind focused on God's plan and promises for your life.

The crying and the complaining must cease. Once you have seen all that is wrong in an area of your life, you must work to maintain a mindset of victory. You have to understand that although this is a trial, it is only temporary. When you think in this manner, it will help you not to focus on the negatives. Instead, it will get your wheels turning on how you can begin to turn that thing around.

Remember, the Lord has already given the promise. Now it's a matter of obtaining the promise. He has made provisions in His Word for assistance when we are having struggles of indecisiveness, inferiority, failure, lack of motivation and all those other shortcomings. Therefore, as good stewards, we must do some troubleshooting and find the scriptures that apply to our particular circumstances and implement the principles therein.

Have you ever gone through something and it looked like there was just no possible way out? You tried every solution you could think of to solve the problem. Then, suddenly, you realized through something someone said or through a scripture you read, that God was and is in control. It just hit you like a ton of bricks (although you know God is omniscient) that God has been in control all along. It's you who's just now figuring out that He has never left.

The Bible says:

James 1:5

> *If any of you lack wisdom, let him ask of God, that giveth to all men liberally, and upbraideth not; and it shall be given him.*

Now, that's a revelation we can all use!

Chapter 7

Tired of Waiting?

Are you impatient? "I want what I want, when I want it and how I want it." It's all the same thing, no matter how you look at it. How many times, as children of the Most High God, do we suffer from this mentality. After all, we've had to wait for one prayer to be fulfilled for so-o-o-o long that it seems like it's never going to happen.

We know what the Bible says:

Proverbs 13:12

Hope deferred maketh the heart sick.

Yes, sometimes we feel sick, sick of waiting, sick of praying, sick of hoping, sick of believing, just sick period. There are so many questions going through our minds. When is God going to move? When will my change come? When will my prayer be answered? I am in it for the long haul, but my goodness, how long will it take for one simple prayer to be answered?

This is not just any prayer, but the one that I really, really want with all my heart. Can God hear me? Have I done something wrong? Do I need to sow another seed of faith? Do I need to go on a fast? What's going on? What is taking so long?

Take a deep breath! Can you relate to all the things I just said? If the truth be told, I know everyone can relate. As human beings, having limited knowledge of our destiny, we are subject to waiting on the plan of God's will to be fulfilled BY FAITH. We can't see it all at once. No matter how badly we want to be in complete control of the plan we have for our lives and the fulfillment of the perfect timeline, God is in control ... if and when you submit your life to His will. Case in point, the Bible says, we prophesy in part, and we know in part:

1 Corinthians 13:9-12

For we know in part, and we prophesy in part. But when that which is perfect comes, then that which is in part shall be done away. When I was a child, I spake as a child, I understood as a child, I thought as a child: but when I became a man, I put away childish things. For now we see through a glass, darkly; but then face to face: now I know in part; but then shall I know even as also I am known.

Tired of Waiting?

If the Lord would allow us to catch a glimpse of our future and how our destiny will unfold, it would be too much for us to handle. Not only that; we, being mortal, would probably sabotage the plan of God because we might think God made a mistake about the decisions He made when He predestined us. We might feel like we know it all and therefore know what's best. After all, God gave us a free will.

At Babel, the people had a plan to reach Heaven. They built what was known as the Tower of Babel in an attempt to reach Heaven. Then, God confused their languages so that they could not communicate. Whether they realized it or not, they were trying to change the course of things. The natural order that God had planned was in jeopardy because of the minds of men. God have given them unity, one language and one speech, but they were not satisfied. They thought that because of their intellect, they could outsmart God.

Genesis 11:1-9

> *And the whole earth was of one language, and of one speech. And it came to pass, as they journeyed from the east, that they found a plain in the land of Shinar; and they dwelt there. And they said one to another, Go to, let us make brick, and burn them thoroughly. And they had brick for stone, and slime had they for mortar. And they said, Go to, let us build us a city and a tower, whose top may reach unto heaven; and let us*

make us a name, lest we be scattered abroad upon the face of the whole earth.

And the LORD came down to see the city and the tower, which the children of men builded. And the LORD said, Behold, the people is one, and they have all one language; and this they begin to do: and now nothing will be restrained from them, which they have imagined to do.

Go to, let us go down, and there confound their language, that they may not understand one another's speech. So the LORD scattered them abroad from thence upon the face of all the earth: and they left off to build the city. Therefore is the name of it called Babel; because the LORD did there confound the language of all the earth: and from thence did the LORD scatter them abroad upon the face of all the earth.

In verse 6, the Lord said, *"Behold, the people are one, and they have all one language; and this they begin to do: and now nothing will be restrained from them, which they have imagined to do."* Wow! The mind of man is so powerful that God had to intervene and stop them from building the tower, or they would have been able to do whatever their mind could conceive of. That's amazing! God could have let them continue on and build that tower, but He knew, in His infinite wisdom, that this was not the best for man. Therefore, He had to stop their plan.

Tired of Waiting?

Even in our world today, men come up with all types of plans and schemes to get more knowledge and go against the plan of God. Many times their plans don't work out because of godly intervention. So it is in your daily life. God loves you enough to thwart the plan you have for your future—if it is on a path that would divert you from His perfect will. The Father had to confuse the steps of the people in Genesis because they were attempting to sabotage His order. The Bible relates:

Psalm 119:133-135

Order my steps in thy word: and let not any iniquity have dominion over me. Deliver me from the oppression of man: so will I keep thy precepts. Make thy face to shine upon thy servant; and teach me thy statutes.

When your steps are ordered by God, you will walk in His perfect will. That means EVERYTHING that God has for you will come to you. WE have to be willing to allow God to say, "NOT NOW!" or "NO!" without us throwing a tantrum. We have to trust that if we allow God to order our steps and direct our paths, things will work out for our good. Knowing the Scriptures and having patience to see them fulfilled is the key. We must stay in the Word of God, for it is our light. He has made preparation in His Word to help us keep looking toward His perfect will for our life.

A God Promise

That even the thoughts of our lives are predestined by God may seem difficult to fathom, but the Bible is true. You were predestined in the heart of God before conception, meaning that God had and has a perfect plan for your life. We often think that there is no way our lives are really predestined by God, but they truly are because God is sovereign. He cannot lie, and He causes all things to work together for our benefit:

Romans 8:28-31

> *And we know that all things work together for good to them that love God, to them who are the called according to his purpose. For whom he did foreknow, he also did predestinate to be conformed to the image of his Son, that he might be the firstborn among many brethren. Moreover whom he did predestinate, them he also called: and whom he called, them he also justified: and whom he justified, them he also glorified. What shall we then say to these things? If God be for us, who can be against us?*

James 1:2-8

> *My brethren, count it all joy when ye fall into divers temptations; knowing this, that the trying of your faith worketh patience. But let patience have her perfect work, that ye may be perfect and entire, wanting nothing. If any of you lack wisdom, let him ask of*

Tired of Waiting?

God, that giveth to all men liberally, and upbraideth not; and it shall be given him.

But let him ask in faith, nothing wavering. For he that wavereth is like a wave of the sea driven with the wind and tossed. For let not that man think that he shall receive any thing of the Lord. A double minded man is unstable in all his ways.

A double-minded person is unstable and changes their mind constantly. Instability is a characteristic that is unlike God. When we're not consistent or stable in our lifestyle and actions, we make our journey more difficult. We actually postpone the fulfillment of God's promises by our contrary behavior. God uses His Word to encourage us to continue on the journey, or path, He has set before us.

Scripture after scripture contains promises from God. For instance:

1 John 1:9

If we confess our sins, he is faithful and just to forgive us our sins, and to cleanse us from all unrighteousness.

This is a promise that if we confess our sins, GOD IS FAITHFUL to forgive us. The Word of God verifies itself. One scripture after another confirms His promises. His Word does not contradict itself.

A God Promise

When you feel impatient and are tired of waiting, remember that everything is in God's timing.

Isaiah 40:31

> *But they that wait upon the* LORD *shall renew their strength; they shall mount up with wings as eagles; they shall run, and not be weary; and they shall walk, and not faint.*

God has put eternity in the heart of man, so that he would not know the beginning from the end:

Ecclesiastes 3:11, NLT

> *Yet God has made everything beautiful for its own time. He has planted eternity in the human heart, but even so, people cannot see the whole scope of God's work from beginning to end.*

Now why did God do that? He did it because He knew that when He created us in His image, man would be inquisitive, curious and determined to gain knowledge and foresight of the future, or what was to come. The Father knew He had to put some limits on man regarding the full knowledge of his destiny. Look at the mentality that Jesus Christ the Son of the living God had. Even though He was and is God, the Scriptures say:

Tired of Waiting?

Philippians 2:5-13

> *Let this mind be in you, which was also in Christ Jesus: who, being in the form of God, thought it not robbery to be equal with God: but made himself of no reputation, and took upon him the form of a servant, and was made in the likeness of men: and being found in fashion as a man, he humbled himself, and became obedient unto death, even the death of the cross. Wherefore God also hath highly exalted him, and given him a name which is above every name: that at the name of Jesus every knee should bow, of things in heaven, and things in earth, and things under the earth; and that every tongue should confess that Jesus Christ is Lord, to the glory of God the Father.*
>
> *Wherefore, my beloved, as ye have always obeyed, not as in my presence only, but now much more in my absence, work out your own salvation with fear and trembling. For it is God which worketh in you both to will and to do of his good pleasure.*

Specifically note that Jesus fashioned Himself as a man, humbled himself, and became obedient unto death, even the death of the cross. Don't you imagine that, as a man, Jesus had questions: "How long do I have to suffer? "When will this end?" "Why do I have to go this route?" "I can't wait until all of this is over." Of course He did, the Scriptures just told you He was found in the fashion of a man, so He had the same feelings and infirmities we do. Always remember that Jesus is our High Priest. He knows when we are suffering, and He is moved with compassion when we sincerely cry out to Him.

Once, when Daniel needed deliverance, he prayed for twenty-one days before relief came. Still, the Bible insists that God heard him on the very first day. Despite his desperation for an answer, Daniel had to continue to wait on God. In the meantime, he did not turn his back on God just because his answer was delayed; he trusted God. An angel told him not to be afraid, that God had heard him the first day he had prayed, and he (the angel) had now come to deliver him because of his prayers to God.

Daniel 10:12

Then said he unto me, Fear not, Daniel: for from the first day that thou didst set thine heart to understand, and to chasten thyself before thy God, thy words were heard, and I am come for thy words.

The angel even told Daniel the reason he was late in coming to his rescue:

Daniel 10:13

But the prince of the kingdom of Persia withstood me one and twenty days: but, lo, Michael, one of the

chief princes, came to help me; and I remained there
with the kings of Persia.

This angel had to call for help in order to get to Daniel and rescue him.

— PRAISE BREAK —
What God won't do for His people!
Just wait on Him!
He shall deliver!

So, here's my point. If Jesus Himself had to submit to the will and timing of God, how much more do we? When we start questioning our life with God and why our prayers are taking so long to be answered, think about Christ's walk on this earth and the fact that He was both God and man. If we could focus on that for just a moment, it might change our perspective on things.

How long have I been wanting a new car? A new house? A husband? How long have I been believing God for a child? How long have I been waiting for healing? For a new business? For money in the bank? For salvation for my family? And on and on and on it goes.

When you look at matters from the right angle, things look different and clearer, the wait doesn't seem as long, the sacrifice doesn't seem as great, and even the pain doesn't seem as intense. At that point, you have reached a crossroads in your walk as a child of God. You have grown to the point you can realize that the world doesn't revolve around your immediate needs.

The plan of God is all inclusive. For example, if you are believing God for a husband or a wife, think of a triangle. You're on the left bottom side of the triangle, and he is on the right side of the triangle or vice versa, and you both pray for "the right one" to enter your lives. You're traveling up the side of the triangle to get to the point (the tip of the triangle) where you can meet each other. The only problem is that the predestined husband is traveling up the side of the triangle at a slower pace than the predestined wife because he's battling doubt and unbelief. Therefore he is experiencing setbacks on his journey, and it's taking him longer to get to the point (the tip of the triangle, the meeting place) to meet his wife.

Maybe the prospective wife is going faster because she's walking in faith, praying and speaking the Word over her life. She gets to the point (the tip of the triangle, the meeting place) first, but now what? She has to wait for her God-ordained husband. He's on the way, but he's not there yet. He has some things to overcome still, but he's working his way there to the promise.

He believes God, and he knows what the Bible says:

Proverbs 18:22, NKJV
He who finds a wife finds a good thing.

He knows he has to find her according to the Word of God. He knows he has to work out his issues because his wife is waiting. He's slowly moving up the side of the triangle. Meanwhile, his prospective wife, already at the top, has been patiently waiting, but now she is getting a little disturbed because it's taking too long. Because she's frustrated and tired of waiting, she starts to go back down the side of the triangle. After some time and more prayer, she goes back to the point (the tip, the meeting place) and decides to continue to stand on the promise of God, knowing that *"the just shall live by faith,"* and she knows that her husband-to-be will find her because the Word is true, and she is in the place that God wants her to be.

The prospective husband works diligently to get there because he knows his gift (promise) awaits. Finally, he is able to resolves his issues, and he sees her in the distance, as he's going up the side. He realizes, "There she is, waiting for me." Then he is ready to claim his promise. After a long journey of roadblocks and challenges, he has made it.

Even though the prospective wife had to get there and wait, the promise was true. If she would have grown weary and gone back or given up, she would not have reaped the promise of God. She had to wait for her husband-to-be to get into position. She could have said, "I'm tired of waiting for him to find me; I'm going to start looking and find my own husband," but surely she would have gotten off the natural course that the Father had laid out for her, and this ultimately would have resulted in unnecessary trials and tribulations.

I gave you this elaborate illustration so that you can understand, child of God, that things don't always line up perfectly as we have imagined them. People don't always have perfect timing. We move at different paces in life, according to how we relate to God. In other words, how we live and manage our life as stewards of the promises of God determines how quickly we receive His promises. When we stay on a path of walking in the Spirit and not in the flesh, we will not prolong our moment of destiny.

Paul wrote to the Galatian believers:

Galatians 5:16-17

> *This I say then, Walk in the Spirit, and ye shall not fulfil the lust of the flesh. For the flesh lusteth against the Spirit, and the Spirit against the flesh: and these are contrary one to the other: so that ye cannot do the things that ye would.*

Oh my! I couldn't have said it better myself. When we walk in the flesh, we cannot receive the things we want from God because we are feeding the flesh. If you want the things of God, you must feed the God (the Holy Spirit) who lives in you, and then all the things you desire shall come to pass because they are God-given. Therefore, you won't live life in a place of "HOPING," but you will transition more into seeing the substance of what you have hope for: a husband, a wife, a new car, a new house, ministry, business, household salvation, etc. Your hope will no longer bring you to a place of being sick because it's taking too long, but you will have discovered the secret of watching your dreams come to pass.

The Bible says:

Hebrews 11:1

Now faith is the substance of things hoped for the evidence of things not seen.

This means: yes, you will be in a state of "hoping" at times, but when your faith is working, you will eventually see the evidence manifest.

When we talk about hope, we are looking at a golden nugget that God gave us to help us hold on to the promise until our faith is fully matured. Hope is like a movie ticket. You see a preview for a movie that you really want to go see on opening night. So, you rush to purchase your ticket because the show may be sold out because it's in such high demand. You go online, hoping to purchase a ticket before they are gone. You are making this effort in the hope of getting to see the movie, and that is the golden nugget that motivates you to wait until the actual ticket to see the movie manifests.

When that ticket finally manifests, the hope you had to see the movie is now turned into faith that you will indeed see the movie (because you have what's necessary in your hand, the ticket, to make you eligible to see the movie). You are no longer hoping. Faith is the evidence of things hoped for. Do you see that?

Again, Paul wrote:

Romans 8:24-25

For we are saved by hope: but hope that is seen is not hope: for what a man seeth, why doth he yet hope for? But if we hope for that we see not, then do we with patience wait for it.

The Lord allows us to see our desires manifest for many different things we have hoped for throughout life, so that we will be encouraged to continue to believe Him for other things.

Allow me to share with you a personal experience. I have two daughters. My oldest daughter's middle name is "FAITH," and the younger daughter's middle name is "HOPE." When I wanted to have children, it didn't happen right away, like I thought it should. I had to make an effort to believe God. The result was not immediate. Therefore, I began to stand on the Scriptures for the first child: *"the just shall live by faith."* I had been saved long enough to know that I couldn't go by what I was seeing. I knew that if I was going to receive the promise of the Lord, I would have to believe in spite of what I was seeing in the natural.

Tired of Waiting?

I began to quote that scripture daily. My faith was strong because I had witnessed so many other miracles in my life already. God had called me to the ministry years before I had my first child, so I was actively ministering and serving in the Kingdom of God. Still, the promise was not automatic. I had to pray and stand and wait. Many times my flesh wanted to give up and get upset because I was doing all the work in the ministry for other people, but I wasn't getting what I wanted personally (at least immediately). I rebuked my flesh and my mind and continued to trust the promise of God:

Psalm 127:3-5

Lo, children are a heritage of the LORD: and the fruit of the womb is his reward. As arrows are in the hand of a mighty man; so are children of the youth. Happy is the man that hath his quiver full of them: they shall not be ashamed, but they shall speak with the enemies in the gate.

I knew that I was eligible to receive this heritage, and that scripture gave me even more faith to believe for the first child. I knew God to be faithful. The psalm declared, in verse 5: *"Happy is the man that has his quiver full of them."* I knew I wanted the happiness of having children, and I knew I would have children. I was just waiting for the timing of God.

A God Promise

By this time, the Lord called my husband and me to leave our home in Louisiana and start a ministry—in Arkansas, of all places. The Lord asking me to move to Arkansas was like asking me to go live in the desert. I did not want to go, and I threw a tantrum at that request. Everything in me rebelled. I did everything I could to change God's mind! I even quoted scriptures to get Him to change His mind. Oh my, how foolish I was!

After months of crying, pouting, complaining and doing every negative, immature thing I could think of, I finally submitted and decided to go. The first day we got to Arkansas, my husband's car was wrecked and totaled. What a way to start the journey! When he called me on the phone to tell me our only vehicle was totaled (and we didn't have insurance at the time), I began to get discouraged. He was devastated. But then I got on my knees and began to pray, he also began to pray over the phone, and immediately the Spirit of God came in the room and gave me these verses:

Psalm 24:7-10

> *Lift up your heads, O ye gates; and be ye lift up, ye everlasting doors; and the King of glory shall come in. Who is this King of glory? The LORD strong and mighty, the LORD mighty in battle. Lift up your heads, O ye gates; even lift them up, ye everlasting doors; and the King of glory shall come in. Who is*

Tired of Waiting?

By that time, I was sobbing so profusely that I was starting to hyperventilate. I knew God had just visited me right then and there–in spite of what things looked like. We had literally been in Arkansas only one day. Nothing like this had happened back in Louisiana, and now this? The natural mind would think we were out of the will of God, but God was saying, "NO! I am with you."

To make a long story short, some weeks later, I was at the new ministry we were starting, the building was freezing cold (about 30 degrees) and snowing), and I had to open up for prayer. I was still getting accustomed to being in Arkansas. For some reason, I felt like a fish out of water there. I didn't know anyone, and it was so cold that I was trembling that night. I was fully dressed and wearing a coat, hat, gloves, earmuffs and boots as I lead the people into prayer.

I felt very disconnected from the prayer and thought it was because of the circumstances. Then, after a couple of minutes, I began to think of how many times God had blessed me and how many times He had spared me. I began to pray for the people and their needs, and suddenly, I was caught up in the presence of God. All of that foolishness and discontent was instantly gone. It was then that I heard the voice of God say to me, "You are pregnant." I stopped praying and began to weep for joy.

A God Promise

When the prayer was over that night, I went home. God had instructed me to get a pregnancy test to check what He had told me, and, sure enough, when I did what the Lord had told me to do, the test was positive. This happened just weeks after we had arrived in Arkansas. Arkansas turned out to be a blessing, and it was God's place to fulfill the promise. As a result of that, we decided that there could be no more fitting name than FAITH for our first child.

The enemy, of course, tried to steal that blessing. During an early doctor's visit, we were told that we should abort this child. This child, he said, would be mentally disabled and might even die of complications. When I heard those words, at first, I sat there trembling. But then I mustered enough strength and courage to rebuke the doctor's words and profess the promises of scripture over my child's life. I never went back to that doctor, and God worked a great miracle for me and our child.

A couple years passed, and we were ready for another child. Again, we had to believe God for a miracle. Before we even began this journey of believing for her to be born, we decided that her name would be HOPE. We didn't know for sure it would be another girl, but we began hoping for another miracle. The hope we had for another blessing kept our faith alive. And again, God was faithful.

As before, the enemy also tried to steal this child. She was very sick. A doctor said it was just a virus and that we should take her home and let the virus run its course. As a mother,

Tired of Waiting?

I knew better. I left that doctor's office and went straight to the emergency room. I knew that my child had something serious, not just a simple virus.

When I got to the ER, we were quickly attended to, nurses came running from different directions, and our baby was immediately admitted with a diagnosis of pneumonia. She spent the next seven days in the hospital, and during that time, my whole life stopped. I entered into a period of fasting and praying. Thankfully, God healed our daughter. Then, on the day Hope was to be released, a nurse gave her a medication that sent all of her vital signs into a downward spiral. Once again, nurses and doctors came running from every direction. I prayed and rebuked death, and God healed our child again. All I can say folks is: GOD IS FAITHFUL TO KEEP HIS PROMISES!

Today both of my daughters are healthy, both were gifted in school, and both are now successful young women. God is good. If I had taken my eyes off of the promise and believed a lie, where would I be today? If I had given up because I was tired of waiting, where would I be? More importantly, where would *they* be? I had to stand in the gap for the promises of God.

Chapter 8

Principles of the Promise

As a steward in the Kingdom of God, you need a plan for success. Yes, I said a plan. Your plan is your road map to walking in victory. Do you realize there are many principles in the Bible to help you be successful? Those principles are your plan for success. If you build on the principles that have already been laid out for you, you can't go wrong. You will have trials and tribulations, but you will overcome every time.

These principles are necessary to keep you focused when temptations, disappointments, persecutions and anything and everything else comes to distract you and destroy you. Those biblical principles will guide you on your journey.

What is a principle? According to the *Oxford Dictionary,* the word *principle* is defined as "a fundamental idea or general rule that is used as a basis for a particular theory or system of belief." As Christians, we stand on the Bible as our system of belief. It contains the tenants of our faith. Therefore, we agree to abide by the truths held within the pages of the Word of God.

When the Father created the world, He set principles in place for the world and all of its inhabitants to abide by. He said in His Word:

Psalm 24:1

> *The earth is the LORD's and the fullness thereof; the world, and they that dwell therein.*

Here are a few of the principles He laid down:

Principle #1: Everything and everyone that is in the Earth belongs to the Lord. He put His creation on notice right away that we all belong to Him. In order to be successful and obtain the promises of God, we must first realize that we are God's.

Ephesians 2:10

> *For we are his workmanship, created in Christ Jesus unto good works, which God hath before ordained that we should walk in them.*

That's right, we are His workmanship, His creation, and the creature is subject to the Creator. Since that is the case, then we, as His creation, must follow His set principles in order to obtain His promises.

Principles of the Promise

The Bible also says:

Acts 17:28

For in him we live, and move, and have our being.

In other words, we cannot operate successfully apart from God. We bloom into everything He ever desired us to be when we walk with Him. We are ordained to succeed and be blessed in Him. That we are in Him means that we have a relationship of prayer, reading the Word and trusting in Him. Can we live separate and apart from Him? Yes, we absolutely can, but if we try, we will never fulfill God's plan for our lives and, most of all, we cannot obtain eternal salvation apart from Him.

We were created for God's pleasure:

Revelation 4:11

Thou art worthy, O Lord, to receive glory and honor and power: for thou hast created all things, and for thy pleasure they are and were created.

Not only did God create us; He created us for His pleasure. This means that He takes pleasure in us. His desire is to see us thriving and happy.

He said in His Word that He wishes above all things that we prosper and be in health even as our soul prospers (see 3 John 1:2). He has made provision for us so that we can obtain His promises. He has given us faith as a tool to walk in His principles. Remember: faith is the substance of what we hope for but do not yet see. When we operate in faith, we acknowledge that God is the Creator and we are His workmanship.

Let's look at that passage again:

Ephesians 2:10

> *For we are his workmanship, created in Christ Jesus unto good works, which God hath before ordained that we should walk in them.*

I've already stated that we are His workmanship, but this scripture adds that we were ordained from the beginning to walk with Him. Amen!

Principle #2: Relax in Him. I know that sounds very simple. Relax in Him? Yes, relax in Him. Let me tell you a quick story that really brings this principle home.

I've always been a very analytical person and somewhat of a perfectionist. For years, I relied on my ability to dissect and investigate any given situation until I could come to a satisfactory conclusion for whatever the scenario was at the time. But what I discovered through the years is that this was a lot of mental and emotional work.

Over-thinking, over-processing things, over-evaluating people and situations can be quite draining. It's just downright exhausting, and it's all rooted in a fear of failure, a fear of what tomorrow may bring, a fear of what people might think. Fear, fear and more fear! A friend of mine would constantly tell me, "RELAX! Stop worrying about how things are going to come out. Stop focusing on if this happens, then what, or if that doesn't happen, then what. Just stop, and relax!" I thought I was just being diligent in how I handled life, but in reality, it was all my insecurities based in fear. It is true that we do have to pay attention in order to make good decisions, but we have to be careful not to sabotage the promise by walking in fear, which creates anxiety and unrest.

In the midst of that admonishment to relax, I could hear the Word of God speaking in my spirit: *"God hath not given us a spirit of fear; but of power, and of love, and of a sound mind"* (2 Timothy 1:7). Although I knew this was true, I had to be told several times— "RELAX!" God was speaking to me directly through my friend: "TRUST ME! WALK BY FAITH! BELIEVE IN THE PROMISE!"

— PRAISE BREAK —

I just said a lot right there. That was two mouthfuls and then some. Fear is not of God. If you believe in the promises of God, at some point, after you have spoken the promise, prayed and believed God for the promise, you must receive the promise. It is when you rest (relax) in Him that you have truly received the promise in your heart of hearts. You know that God is faithful to do what He said He would do, and you no longer have to mull over and rehearse things repeatedly to have a sense of peace about a particular matter. You can have peace at every juncture because you're standing on His Word, and you can relax in Him.

Principle #3: Forgive Yourself. Many of you may be familiar with the scripture that says, *"For all have sinned and come short of the glory of God"* (Romans 3:23). This scripture makes it clear that *"all"* of mankind has failed to meet the Father's expectations of holiness and righteousness. We do not have the ability in our own selves to be holy. We CANNOT be holy without the shed BLOOD OF JESUS CHRIST.

As we have seen, David wrote in Psalms 51, after having sinned with Bathsheba: *"Behold I was shapen in iniquity; and in sin did my mother conceive me. Behold, thou desirest truth in the inward parts; and in the hidden part thou shalt make me to know wisdom. Purge me with hyssop, and I shall be clean; wash me, and I shall be whiter than snow."*

WE WERE ALL BORN IN SIN, FOLKS! That's why we need a Savior. And yet this same David who needed forgiveness was *"a man after his [God's] own heart,"* according to the Word of God (1 Samuel 13:14). In the book of Romans, the apostle Paul describes the dilemma that we are faced with when we want to do good but evil is present:

Principles of the Promise

Romans 7:19-25

For the good that I would, I do not; but the evil which I would not, that I do. Now if I do that I would not, it is no more I that do it, but sin that dwelleth in me. I find then a law, that, when I would do good, evil is present with me. For I delight in the law of God after the inward man; but I see another law in my members, warring against the law of my mind, and bringing me into captivity to the law of sin which is in my members. O wretched man that I am! Who shall deliver me from the body of this death? I thank God through Jesus Christ our Lord. So then with the mind, I myself serve the law of God; but with the flesh the law of sin.

What profound scriptures! This is the story of man in a constant warfare to put the flesh under subjection to the Spirit. And this is why we MUST WALK IN THE SPIRIT, so that we don't fulfill the lusts of the flesh.

Romans 8:1-4

There is therefore now no condemnation to them which are in Christ Jesus, who walk not after the flesh, but after the Spirit. For the law of the Spirit of life in Christ Jesus hath made me free from the law of sin and death. For what the law could not do, in that it was weak through the flesh, God sending his

A God Promise

*own Son in the likeness of sinful flesh, and for sin,
condemned sin in the flesh; that the righteousness of
the law might be fulfilled in us, who walk not after
the flesh, but after the Spirit.*

Here Paul was exhorting the members of the early Church
not to condemn themselves for sin because once you accept
Jesus Christ as your personal Savior, you can go boldly to
the throne of grace to find help in time of need. You can
find forgiveness because Jesus' shed blood made the provision for our redemption to God. It is the POWER of the
BLOOD OF JESUS and the PRESENCE of the HOLY
SPIRIT that gives us the ability to overcome our flesh and
walk in the Spirit.

FORGIVE yourselves, saints of God. So many of us are
walking around bound, not because God has not forgiven
us, but because we have not forgiven ourselves for sins we
committed in the past, things we are ashamed of or embar-
rassed about, or sometimes even sins that were committed
against us. Some of the sins of your past or your present
haunt you throughout the day and even when you're trying
to rest at night. I want you to know that this is a favorite
tactic of Satan.

God loves you, and because He is God, He knows all
about your sin. But He also knows your heart. You must fall
on your face before God and forgive yourself so that you can
believe Him for the promises. If not, you don't have to worry

about the devil coming against you; you will sabotage and disqualify yourself from receiving all that God has for you.

PRINCIPLE #4: Live life like God is your Daddy. This is my favorite part. When you have been redeemed, justified and sanctified, you can live life like God is your Daddy. Why? Because, clearly you have it all. You have everything you need to live the God-kind of life. At this stage in your life, your relationship is so intimate with the Father that He is no longer just God; He is Daddy. He is the One you can count on and depend on. He will be there when you need Him.

When I was a little girl, my brothers and sister and I used to wait for our dad to get home because he always brought us something, whether it was cookies, candy or just a big hug and a spin in the air. The anticipation of him coming home was one thing, but him actually bringing us a gift or something he had promised was icing on the cake.

Why were we so excited? Because he was Daddy. We believed him, and we loved him. As children of the Most High, we do not yet, at any one point, have all that we are believing for, but we are always in a state of believing as we grow. Everything may not have manifested tangibly yet, but you can know that it is coming. What's even greater is that you know the One who's making it all happen: Abba, Father, Daddy! As I mentioned earlier in the text, He promises:

A God Promise

1 Corinthians 2:9, NKJV

*Eye has not seen, nor ear heard, nor have entered into
the heart of man the things which God has prepared
for those who love him.*

MY INTERPRETATION: "YOU CAN'T EVEN BE-
GIN TO IMAGINE WHAT GOD HAS PREPARED
FOR YOU!"

— PRAISE BREAK —

How exciting is that? I don't have to live a life of gloom
and doom, death and destruction! I can live a life of expecta-
tion. I can live a victorious life. I don't want to just live my
best life; I want to live a God-kind of life. My best life can't
touch the kind of life God has for me. I'm sure my best life
would not even compare to the plans Daddy has for me.
After all, He is Jehovah-Jireh, my Provider. I trust that He
will provide, not only what I need. As I serve Him with all
my heart, He will also provide the things that I want.

I want everything Daddy has to give—spiritually, men-
tally, emotionally and physically. I commit to living out loud.
I'm going to live like God is my Daddy because He is, and
I'm not going to make any excuse for it.

Make no mistake about it: there will be highs and lows
in your life, because that's the nature of life. Everything in
God flows in seasons:

Principles of the Promise

Ecclesiastes 3:1-3

> *To every thing there is a season, and a time to every purpose under the heaven; a time to be born, a and a time to die; a time to plant, and a time to pluck up that which is planted; a time to kill, and a time to heal; a time to break down, and a time to build up.*

As you grow in your walk with God, you will be mature enough to go through the periods of ups and downs and still recognize that you are truly blessed because of your relationship with the Father. He has made so many provisions for us that I used to wonder: Why were we so important to Him? I really used to wonder: Why did God care? I wondered: Why did it matter? Why was it so crucial that we know God and the pardoning of our sins? Then one day, it hit me like a ton of bricks when I read Psalm 8:

Psalm 8:4-6

> *What is man that thou art mindful of him? and the son of man, that thou visitest him? For thou hast made him a little lower than the angels, and hast crowned him with glory and honor. Thou madest him to have dominion over the works of thy hands; thou hast put all things under his feet.*

Now, if I'm crowned with glory and honor and I have dominion over the works of God's hands, and all things

A God Promise

are under my feet, I'm supposed to live life like God is my Daddy—because He is!

When the Father created us in His image, He created us to take dominion in the earth. He created His people to make a difference everywhere we go. Jesus said:

Matthew 5:14-16

> *Ye are the light of the world. A city that is set on a hill cannot be hid. Neither do men light a candle, and put it under a bushel, but on a candlestick; and it giveth light unto all that are in the house. Let your light so shine before men, that they may see your good works, and glorify your Father which is in heaven.*

God has given you a light that is meant to SHINE. It is designed for men to see so that they will be drawn to the Light. When men see your light, that's your opportunity to tell them where the light comes from, so that you can both glorify God.

I have a testimony regarding this very issue. Years ago, I worked for the United States Postal Service in the Mark-Up Unit. At the time, I was an eager beaver for Jesus. I was pumped up and excited every day about my salvation. I had not gone through many trials yet because I was new in God. Every day, when I went to work, the same lady and I stood next to each other inputting and sorting mail, and she would tell stories about her family and her ambitions, and

I would talk about Jesus. The next day she would come in and talk about her family and her ambitions, and I would talk about Jesus. And again, she would come in and talk about her family and her ambitions, and I would talk about Jesus. One day, after about two years of this, she suddenly broke down as we were sorting mail and confessed to me, "Stephanie, I'm so jealous of you."

I was shocked and asked her why. It seemed like she had everything a person could want—a house, a car, money, a family, etc. I was fresh out of high school and not even married yet. I didn't have much money, and I had no children and no tangible evidence of success. Why was this woman jealous of me?

When she told me that she was jealous of me because of my relationship with Jesus, I was floored. I asked her if I could pray for her that she could have a relationship with God just like I did, and right there, she accepted Christ as her Lord and Savior. That's what it's all about!

Chapter 9

Even When Other People Are Not with You

God's promises are not contingent upon any man or woman being in agreement with you to make it happen for you. God does not need your friends, your family, your husband or your wife to stand in agreement with you for you to receive YOUR PROMISE. The promises God makes to His Bride are personal to each and every one of us. When we grab hold of a promise for our life, we stand on it until it comes to pass—no matter what anyone else thinks or believes because that promises is specifically for us:

2 Corinthians 9:8

> *And God is able to make all grace abound toward you, that you, always having all sufficiency in all things, may have an abundance for every good work.*

A God Promise

In other words, because God is sovereign, He gives us the grace we need so that we are able to receive His promises. God's grace is not reliant upon man's commitment. Although men can express love, concern, commitment, loyalty and the like, men CANNOT fulfill the promises of God. This is God's doing alone, and God does not want His people looking to another person to provide His promises.

WOW! I said something important right there! Although, the Lord can use people, He does not ever want us (His people) putting our hope and our trust in others for the promise. We should always know that God is our Deliverer, Healer, Provider, Waymaker, Comforter and Friend.

God can cause a person to do something for you (wholeheartedly or even reluctantly) to fulfill a promise He made to you, and many times that person doesn't even know why they have done it. They may not have a relationship with God, and they are simply a vessel God used to fulfill His purpose.

When we look to man, we forget that God is the Source. It is true that people are often the bearers of the promise— whether it's a job offer, a loan, a love offering, a new house, a listening ear, etc.—but it is God who puts it in their heart to do it.

Romans 8:28, NKJV

And we know that all things work together for good to those who love God, to those who are the called according to His purpose.

Even When Other People Are Not with You

Brothers and sisters, it is GOD who allows all things to work together for your good. He orchestrates your blessing. He arranges situations to meet your needs (when the fullness of time has come). The Bible says:

Psalm 30:5

Weeping may endure for a night, but joy cometh in the morning.

You will have to go through trials and tribulations, defeats and failures, but just know that they are only temporary. Your trials may last through the night, but eventually morning will come. Thank God, His mercies are new every morning:

Lamentations 3:22-23

It is of the LORD's mercies that we are not consumed, because his compassions fail not. They are new every morning: great is thy faithfulness.

Hallelujah! What a God we serve, Who gives us NEW mercies EVERY morning! He is a magnificent, omniscient and ever loving God.

— PRAISE BREAK —

A God Promise

I said to you earlier in this chapter that God's promises are not reliant upon other people. Allow me to expound on that thought a little. Although God does use other people to be the bearers of the (tangible) promises, He does not need them to agree to fulfill the promise. In His sovereignty, God can use whom He chooses to cause His Word to come to pass. Remember the promise:

Isaiah 55:11
So shall my word be that goeth forth out of my mouth: it shall not return unto me void, but it shall accomplish that which I please, and it shall prosper in the thing whereto I sent it.

When the Lord put all of these provisions in place, they actually come out of His character as God. You might ask, "How can you say that?" Well, let's look at some of the names of God. They reveal His character. Therefore, when we look at His names, we can see the Father in a spiritual light. His names allow us to experience the many facets of His character. All of these aspects of the Father allow us to be more than conquerors through Christ Jesus. We are totally reliant upon Him.

Jehovah-Rapha

Jehovah-Rapha (*yeh-ho-vaw' raw-faw*) means the Lord Who Heals (see Exodus 15:26). We experience Jehovah-Rapha when we are in need of healing. Many times we quote Isaiah 53:5, *"With his stripes we are healed,"* to indicate that we believe for the promise of healing. It is the LORD OUR HEALER you are speaking to when you pray for healing.

Jehovah-Jireh

Jehovah-Jireh (*yeh-ho-yaw' yire-eh*) means the Lord our Provider (see Genesis 22:14). We experience Jehovah-Jireh when we need our daily needs met, when we need a financial blessing, we need a door to be opened in our life, or we need to find a way out. When we pray the words of Matthew 6:11, *"Give us this day our daily bread,"* (part of what we call the Lord's Prayer) we are speaking of GOD OUR PROVIDER!

Jehovah-Shalom

Jehovah-Shalom (*yeh-ho-vaw' shaw-lome'*) means the Lord our Peace (see Judges 6:24). We meet Jehovah-Shalom when we are at the end of our rope. Many times, when we are distraught, depressed, feeling alone, fearful, defeated and unable to rest at night, it is then we need the presence of Jehovah Shalom—GOD OUR PEACE! When you pray the words of Philippians 4:7, *"And the peace of God, which passeth all understanding, shall keep your hearts and minds through Christ Jesus,"* you are speaking of Jehovah-Shalom.

A God Promise

Jehovah-Chereb

Jehovah-Chereb (*yeh-ho-vaw' che reb*) means the Lord our Sword (see Deuteronomy 33:29). We can see Jehovah-Chereb when we need God's help in a time of trouble. He protects us from adverse circumstances in our lives. Deuteronomy 33:29, gives a clearer picture of Jehovah Chereb:

Blessed are you, Israel!
Who is like you, a people saved by the LORD [Jehovah]?
He is your shield and helper and your glorious sword [Chereb]. (NKJV)

People don't speak of this characteristic of God often because we are uncomfortable about speaking of our enemies and their due justice, but God has said:

Psalm 37:1-2

Fret not thyself because of evildoers, neither be thou envious against the workers of iniquity. For they shall soon be cut down like the grass, and wither as the green herb.

Psalm 37:7-10

Rest in the LORD, and wait patiently for him: fret not thyself because of him who prospereth in his way, because of the man who bringeth wicked devices to pass. Cease from anger, and forsake wrath: fret not thyself in any wise to do evil. For evildoers shall be cut off: but those that wait upon the LORD, they shall inherit the earth. For yet a little while, and the wicked shall not be: yea, thou shalt diligently consider his place, and it shall not be.

Psalm 37:12-14

The wicked plotteth against the just, and gnasheth upon him with his teeth. The LORD shall laugh at him: for he seeth that his day is coming. The wicked have drawn out the sword, and have bent their bow, to cast down the poor and needy, and to slay such as be of upright conversation.

Yes, He is our Jehovah-Chereb.

Jehovah-Machsi

Jehovah-Machsi *(yeh-ho-vaw' mee-shi)* means the Lord my Refuge. I think this aspect of God is the one that we see most. God is our Refuge. How many times have we had to take refuge in God when the circumstances of life were too great for us to handle? How many times have we prayed for divine protection and safety when the enemy surrounded us on all sides? JEHOVAH-MACHSI is well known to the people of God.

A God Promise

Psalm 91 is one of the most quoted and prayed passages of scripture in the entire Bible. Verses 9-10 of that psalm says, *"If you say, The LORD [Jehovah] is my refuge [Machsi]," and you make the Most High your dwelling; there shall no evil befall thee, neither shall any plague come nigh thy dwelling"* (NIV). That is our Jehovah-Machsi.

In the next three names of God, we see the Godhead (Trinity):

Ab

'Ab *(ob)* means God our Father (see Psalm 68:5). We recognize and honor God our Father when we declare that we are not our own, but we were bought with a price on Calvary. We acknowledge 'AB when calling Him "Father."

Romans 8:14-17

> *For as many as are led by the Spirit of God, they are the sons of God. For ye have not received the spirit of bondage again to fear; but ye have received the Spirit of adoption, whereby we cry, Abba, Father. The Spirit itself beareth witness with our spirit, that we are the children of God: and if children, then heirs; heirs of God, and joint-heirs with Christ; if so be that we suffer with him, that we may be also glorified together.*

As stated in Psalm 68:5: *"A father of the fatherless, and a judge of the widows, is God in his holy habitation."*

Jehovah-Elohim (Yeshua)

Jehovah-Elohim (Yeshua) is the Son of God, Jesus (see Matthew 16:16). Simon Peter answered Jesus, *"You are the Christ the Son of the living God [Elohim]."* Of course, we see Jesus throughout the entirety of the New Testament as He fulfilled His divine call to redeem man back to God. He is our Jehovah-Elohim.

He is the Son of God, as seen in John 6:

John 6:33-39

For the bread of God is he which cometh down from heaven, and giveth life unto the world.

Then said they unto him, Lord, evermore give us this bread.

And Jesus said unto them, I am the bread of life: he that cometh to me shall never hunger; and he that believeth on me shall never thirst. But I said unto you, That ye also have seen me, and believe not. All that the Father giveth me shall come to me; and him that cometh to me I will in no wise cast out. For I came down from heaven, not to do my own will, but the will of him that sent me. And this is the Father's will which hath sent me, that of all which he hath

*given me I should lose nothing, but should raise it
up again at the last day.*

I encourage you to read John 6 in its entirety as it reveals
God's plan from the beginning to provide Jesus as the pro-
pitiation for the sins of every man. The provision of Jehovah
Elohim Yeshua (Jesus) is the promise of God the Father to
all those who believe.

A PRAYER OF SALVATION

If you're reading this book today, you don't know Jesus as
your Lord and Savior and you want to know Him, all you
have to do is say this prayer after me:

> Lord, I come to You in the name of Your
> Son, Jesus. Forgive me of my sins. Wash
> me in His precious blood. I acknowledge
> that He died on the cross to redeem me
> back to God. I believe that He is the Sav-
> ior of the world. Today, I believe that I am
> saved, and I accept Jesus as Lord and
> Savior of my life.
>
> Amen!

There is one final name of God that I want to explore here:

Ruach Hakkodesh, Holy Spirit (see Acts 2)

The Holy Spirit is well known for His manifestation in the book of Acts:

Acts 2:1-4

> *And when the day of Pentecost was fully come, they were all with one accord in one place. And suddenly there came a sound from heaven as of a rushing mighty wind, and it filled the house where they were sitting. And there appeared unto them cloven tongues like fire, and it sat upon each of them. And they were all filled with the Holy Ghost, and began to speak with other tongues, as the Spirit gave them utterance.*

We have experienced the Holy Spirit moving in our churches and in our own personal lives so many times, but the Holy Spirit is more than a manifestation. He is God. We know that He is Power and Comfort. He is the Guide of our life. He lives within us to help us to fulfill the call of God on our lives. We cannot do it without Him. He is God in us now.

When Jesus left the earth, He sent the Holy Spirit to dwell and abide in us, to let us know that we are not alone. The Holy Spirit is there for us. Look at what the Scriptures say about the Holy Spirit, the Spirit of Truth:

A God Promise

John 16:7-14

Nevertheless I tell you the truth; It is expedient for you that I go away: for if I go not away, the Comforter will not come unto you; but if I depart, I will send him unto you. And when he is come, he will reprove the world of sin, and of righteousness, and of judgment: of sin, because they believe not on me; of righteousness, because I go to my Father, and ye see me no more; of judgment, because the prince of this world is judged.

I have yet many things to say unto you, but ye cannot bear them now.

Howbeit when he, the Spirit of truth, is come, he will guide you into all truth: for he shall not speak of himself; but whatsoever he shall hear, that shall he speak: and he will shew you things to come. He shall glorify me: for he shall receive of me, and shall shew it unto you.

Aren't you glad we know this wonderful God!

Chapter 10

Make a Promise to Yourself!

All right, family of God, this is where the hardest part comes in. You have to make a promise to yourself to BELIEVE GOD. We already know that it will not be easy. We know there will be trials and tribulations, hurdles and obstacles, highs and lows, ups and downs, but in the midst of it all, YOU MUST STAND. YOU MUST HOLD ON TO THE PROMISE.

Remember, as a child of God, your journey will be filled with believing and waiting for God's promises to manifest. As soon as one promise is fulfilled, you will be faced with believing for another promise (depending on your circumstances). The Word of God encourages us to put on the whole armor of God to be able to stand against the wiles of the enemy. This armor is key to daily victories. You will be vulnerable at times. That's why it is so important to put on the armor, to protect yourself against all the attacks that will come your way.

A God Promise

Let's take a look at the elements of the armor of God. Just as a soldier would wear armor to protect himself, the armor of God is spiritual protection for the believer. What does the armor represent? How does it work? How does it help us to overcome evil? Why should we put on the whole armor? The apostle Paul encourages us in this way:

Ephesians 6:10-17

> *Finally, my brethren, be strong in the Lord, and in the power of his might. Put on the whole armour of God, that ye may be able to stand against the wiles of the devil. For we wrestle not against flesh and blood, but against principalities, against powers, against the rulers of the darkness of this world, against spiritual wickedness in high places. Wherefore take unto you the whole armour of God, that ye may be able to withstand in the evil day, and having done all, to stand.*
> *Stand therefore, having your loins girt about with truth, and having on the breastplate of righteousness; and your feet shod with the preparation of the gospel of peace; above all, taking the shield of faith, wherewith ye shall be able to quench all the fiery darts of the wicked. And take the helmet of salvation, and the sword of the Spirit, which is the word of God.*

HAVING YOUR LOINS GIRT WITH THE BELT OF TRUTH

You are living a life of truth, honesty and integrity. You know the Father's voice. In essence, when you wear the belt of truth, you are declaring that you are walking in truth. You will not deceive others or be deceived by the enemy's schemes.

As I stated earlier, the Word of God says:

John 10:4-5

And when he putteth forth his own sheep, he goeth before them, and the sheep follow him: for they know his voice. And a stranger will they not follow, but will flee from him: for they know not the voice of strangers.

You walk in truth because you know the Father's voice, and you are in communion with Him. He will protect you when any other voice tries to get you off track. He will reveal the wolf in sheep's clothing to you ... if you are walking in truth. This is the basic principle of this part of the armor.

Allow me to interject something here for absolute clarity: because the Father is sovereign, He can bless you because of His mercy and grace. These scriptures are principles that we live by as we strive to be good stewards of God's Word, but at no time is God limited because we forgot to apply a principle. He knows our heart's desire to be like Him and serve Him in honesty and integrity.

PUTTING ON THE BREASTPLATE OF RIGHTEOUSNESS

When we put on this breastplate, it is an indicator that we know we have been bought with a price. We are the righteousness of God through Christ Jesus, but because there is no righteousness in us, we must wear the breastplate of righteousness whereby Jesus' blood represents our righteousness:

2 Corinthians 5:21, AMPC

For our sake He made Christ [virtually] to be sin Who knew no sin, so that in and through Him we might become [endued with, viewed as being in, and examples of] the righteousness of God [what we ought to be, approved and acceptable and in right relationship with Him, by His goodness].

At the time of salvation, we receive the breastplate of righteousness. It is designed to guard our soul and heart from deception and evil. We put it on by seeking God and His righteousness. Making Him and His ways our dwelling place, we delight in His commands and desire for His ways to become our ways. When God reveals to us an area in which we need to change, we should obey Him and allow Him to do what is necessary. When we don't listen to the Spirit, we give Satan the opportunity to penetrate the armor. Obedience is key. As we practice being in God's presence, we begin to develop a pureness in heart, which causes us to live a godly life.

HAVING YOUR FEET SHOD WITH PREPARATION OF THE GOSPEL OF PEACE

Having your *"feet shod"* means that your feet are protected. In essence, as we travel our life's journey, we walk in the peace of the Word of God, and He orders our steps. The protection of our feet, our feet being covered, gives us the endurance to continue on the journey in spite of the rough and dangerous roads we must travel. It also keeps us focused on our path of righteousness and destiny.

TAKING UP THE SHIELD OF FAITH

The shield of faith guards us from the fiery darts the enemy throws at us through various temptations. You can see the works of the flesh in Galatians 5:

Galatians 5:19-21

Now the works of the flesh are manifest, which are these; Adultery, fornication, uncleanness, lasciviousness, idolatry, witchcraft, hatred, variance,

*emulations, wrath, strife, seditions, heresies, envy-
ings, murders, drunkenness, revellings, and such like:
of the which I tell you before, as I have also told you
in time past, that they which do such things shall
not inherit the kingdom of God.*

When faced with a temptation, we have to decide whether
we will obey God or follow the lusts of our flesh. The temptation is like fiery dart the enemy sends your way. That ole'
Slewfoot will come to you just as he tried to tempt Jesus in
the wilderness. He will tell you all the reasons you should
follow his suggestions to sin. He will try to convince you by
all means necessary to do the wrong things.

For example, he will bring thoughts like: "I'm tired of
waiting on God," "what's the use," "it's okay if I sin this one
time," "I can always repent." These thoughts are contrary to
the will of God for your life. We have to stand up and use
the Word against Satan, just as Jesus did, and those fiery
darts will bounce off of the Shield of Faith and return void
to the sender—Satan.

TAKING THE HELMET OF SALVATION

Soldiers wear helmets to protect their head from being
injured. A helmet is important because in battle, attacks can
come from any direction in the form of flying debris, holes

Make a Promise to Yourself!

in the ground that can cause you to fall, etc. As Christians, our helmet protects us against demonic spiritual wickedness in high places. Every day the devil and his imps are on their job, to rob us and destroy us. Your helmet is structured to resist anything that comes flying through the air to make an impact upon your head.

The Bible says that we should have the mind of Christ (see 1 Corinthians 2:16). When we put on that helmet of salvation, it reminds us that we have the mind of Christ. Therefore, unbelief cannot infiltrate our mind and cause us to walk in doubt and unbelief.

Doubt and unbelief bring discouragement, which brings defeat. When we walk in doubt and unbelief, we are giving power to Satan to get us off track and destroy our life. As you will see, when you stop walking in faith and begin to walk in doubt and unbelief, everything that can go wrong will go wrong. Child of God, you must wear your helmet. Keep your mind stayed on Jesus:

Philippians 4:8

> *Finally, brethren, whatsoever things are true, whatsoever things are honest, whatsoever things are just, whatsoever things are pure, whatsoever things are lovely, whatsoever things are of good report; if there be any virtue, and if there be any praise, think on these things.*

WIELDING THE SWORD OF THE SPIRIT

A soldier's sword was used in battle to make direct contact and destroy the enemy. Because of its sharpness, it could penetrate the flesh of a man and kill him. It was a powerful natural weapon.

A Christian's sword is a spiritual weapon—the Word God. The Bible says:

Hebrews 4:12

> *For the word of God is quick, and powerful, and sharper than any twoedged sword, piercing even to the dividing asunder of soul and spirit, and of the joints and marrow, and is a discerner of the thoughts and intents of the heart.*

When we use our sword against the enemy in our daily battles, he cannot win. Just as Jesus defeated him in the wilderness (and on so many other occasions) with the Word, we will have the same victory when we implement the Word of God in our daily life and prayer time. The Sword of the Spirit is essential to our success as Christians.

— PRAISE BREAK —
Praise God that His armor is available to you! Put it all on!

Chapter 11

Once the Promise Is Fulfilled

After all has been said and done, and God has once again fulfilled another promise to you, please remember the following:

- Acknowledge God
- Testify to Others
- Thank and Praise God
- Give to God's work
- THEN DO IT ALL AGAIN (for the next promise)!

ACKNOWLEDGE GOD

How do we acknowledge God? Psalms 100 makes it plain:

Psalm 100:1-5

> *Make a joyful noise unto the LORD, all ye lands.*
> *Serve the LORD with gladness: come before his pres-*

ence with singing. Know ye that the LORD he is God: It is he that hath made us, and not we ourselves; we are his people and the sheep of his pasture. Enter into his gates with thanksgiving, and into his courts with praise; be thankful unto him, and bless his name. For the LORD is good; his mercy is everlasting; and his truth endureth to all generations.

When we acknowledge God, we are recognizing that He is worthy of all praise. The Bible tells us that when the people of God talk about the works of God, He listens and He remembers:

Malachi 3:16

Then they feared the LORD spake often one to another; and the LORD hearkened and heard it, and a book of remembrance was written before him for them that feared the LORD, and that thought upon his name.

Acknowledging God is key. In this way, we let the Lord know that we recognize Him, we honor Him and we adore him.

TESTIFY TO OTHERS
(TELL SOMEBODY WHAT GOD HAS DONE FOR YOU!)

Why should I tell someone what God has done for me? The tongue has the power of life and death:

Proverbs 18:21

Death and life are in the power of the tongue: and they that love it shall eat the fruit thereof.

In other words, when you speak words of victory over your life, it determines your outcome, and you will be the benefactor of the blessings. The Bible also says:

Revelation 12:11

And they overcame him by the blood of the Lamb, and by the word of their testimony; and they loved not their lives unto the death.

Along with the blood of Christ, your words cause you to walk in the victory that God has ordained for you. The words of your mouth are powerful. Just consider how the Lord spoke the world into existence and all that is in it before it manifested. He didn't labor to make it happen; He just spoke it, and it was.

Although we are made of flesh and live in a natural world, we live by faith. Therefore, we practice our faith when we speak the Word of God over our life. When we tell of God's goodness, we are letting people know that God is our Source. We're letting them know that we thrive and excel in life when we serve God. When we use our words, we are simply mirroring God because we are made in His image. What comes out of our mouth is a tool that God has given us to direct our life's path.

Your testimony is everything. I don't now know many times someone else's story has impacted my life and become the catalyst for change in me. You must testify of God's goodness. It is a powerful weapon against the wiles of the enemy. Every time you testify of what God has done, you shoot another arrow through the plan of Satan. His imps begin to get confused. His schemes for your life fall apart. Then, he must fall into the ditch he dug for you and yours. Praise God! Testify, saints!

Read the story below entitled "Jesus Cleanses a Leper":

Mark 1:40-45, NKJV

Now a leper came to Him, imploring Him, kneeling down to Him and saying to Him, "If you are willing, you can make me clean." Then Jesus, moved with compassion, stretched out His hand and touched him, and said to him, "I am willing; be cleansed." As soon as he had spoken, immediately the leprosy left him, and he was cleansed.

And he strictly warned him and sent him away at once, and said to him, "See that you say nothing to anyone; but go your way, show yourself to the priest, and offer for your cleansing those things which Moses commanded, as a testimony to them." However, he went out and began to proclaim it freely, and to spread the matter, so that Jesus could no longer openly enter the city, but was outside in deserted places; and they came to Him from every direction.

There was a direct impact made on other people as a result of the leper's testimony of Jesus healing him. When we testify and thank God for what He has done, men are drawn to Him. The result is that more people have the opportunity to come to Christ.

As the Bible declares, when we lift up Jesus, all men will be drawn unto him (see John 12:32). Testifying is a tool that is used to win lost souls to Christ, so it is important that we tell of God's goodness when we have received a miracle from Him.

Notice in the following passages that Jesus was sought after when He returned home to Israel. The people still were drawn to Him because of His works in the land. There was so much talk about Jesus coming home that there *"was no room left, not even outside the door."* If Jesus was going to preach, the people wanted to hear it. They, too, wanted to experience Jesus.

A God Promise

Jesus Forgives and Heals a Paralyzed Man
Mark 2:1-5, NIV

> *A few days later, when Jesus again entered Capernaum, the people heard that he had come home. They gathered in such large numbers that there was no room left, not even outside the door, and he preached the word to them. Some men came, bringing to him a paralyzed man, carried by four of them. Since they could not get him to Jesus because of the crowd, they made an opening in the roof above Jesus by digging through it and then lowered the mat the man was lying on. When Jesus saw their faith, he said to the paralyzed man, "Son, your sins are forgiven."*

The Lord Jesus moved in such mighty ways during that day. However, just as the people testified then and spread the word of Jesus' coming, we ought to do the same today when we have the opportunity to share the Good News.

GIVE TO GOD'S WORK

It is imperative that we support the work of God by giving of our time and resources. The Lord always has an example for us to follow as Christians. Lydia was a great example of this in the book of Acts. She was a businesswoman who sold purple cloth. She was a diligent worker and, therefore, very wealthy. She accepted Christ through Paul's ministry and, ultimately, became a great resource for the work of Christ during that time.

Not only did Lydia give of her wealth; she also opened her home to the apostles Paul and Silas when they were released from prison. Her home was always open for the work of the ministry. There is great speculation that one of the first churches in Philippi may have started in her home. Lydia served God with all that she had, and as a result, she continued to be blessed.

Here is her testimony:

Acts 16:13-15, NIV

> *On the Sabbath we went outside the city gate to the river, where we expected to find a place of prayer. We sat down and began to speak to the women who had gathered there. One of those listening was a woman from the city of Thyatira named Lydia, a dealer in purple cloth. She was a worshiper of God. The Lord opened her heart to respond to Paul's message. When she and the members of her household were baptized, she invited us to her home. "If you consider me a believer in the Lord," she said, "come and stay at my house." And she persuaded us.*

A God Promise

I challenge you today to be like Lydia. Give God your all and your absolute best, and be open to how the Father wants to use you to support His work and His people. You can't go wrong when you apply the principle of giving to the work of God.

— PRAISE BREAK —
Hallelujah to God!
He is a Promise Keeper!

Closing

In closing, I pray that this book has increased your knowledge of how to receive the promises of God in your life. Just know that the Father loves you with an unconditional love and has the best in mind for you. He has a plan and a purpose for your life, and He will give you access to everything you need to fulfill your purpose. As you walk in Him and put Him first, He will surely reward you by giving you the desires of your heart.

Did you know that when you are one with Christ, your desires become aligned with the Father's because you are dying to the flesh daily? With that in mind, Child of God, be encouraged, be faithful, be patient and wait on your promises.

God's Best Blessings Be Upon You,

Stephanie

Author Contact Page

You may contact the author, Stephanie S. Johnson, in the following ways:

Cell: 504-421-3976
Email: THEGIVINGPLACELOUISIANA@gmail.com
Email: Aplustutoring2013@gmail.com
Website: TheGivingPlaceLouisiana.com
Facebook: The Giving Place

Other Books by
Stephanie Johnson

Life Lessons

of the
Good Teacher

Overcoming Life's Obstacles:
The Wilderness Season

Stephanie S. Johnson, M.Ed.

Help, I'm Being Bullied

Another title in the series: *The Adventures of Jeremy Jackson, Wisdom Seeker*

Written by Stephanie Johnson, M.Ed.
Illustrated by Brittani Landry

"A Two Elle's Story"